Home Remodeling: Walls, Windows & Doors

Handyman Club Library™

Minneapolis, Minnesota

Home Remodeling: Walls, Windows & Doors

CREDITS

Mike Vail
Vice President, Products & Business Development

Tom Carpenter
Director of Books & New Media Development

Mark Johanson
Book Products Development Manager
Handyman Club of America

Dan Cary
Senior Book Production Assistant

Chris Marshall
Editorial Coordinator

Gary Branson, Mark Johanson, Chris Marshall
Writers

Bill Nelson
Series Design, Art Direction and Production

Mark Macemon
Lead Photographer

Kim Bailey
Photography

John Nadeau, Troy Johnson, Tom Deveny
Technical Advisors and Builders

Craig Claeys
Contributing Illustrator

Dan Kennedy
Book Production Manager

PHOTO CREDITS

Pages 7, 9
Craftmaster Doors
Pages 11, 120, 127
Peachtree Doors & Windows
Pages 7, 8, 9, 10
Pella Corp.
Page 10
Premwood Doors
Pages 11, 120
Semco Windows & Doors
Pages 10, 84
Velux-America, Inc.

ISBN 1-58159-000-8

Handyman Club of America
12301 Whitewater Drive
Minnetonka, Minnesota 55343

Table of Contents

Home Remodeling: Walls, Windows & Doors

Introduction

When we think of home remodeling, the first image that usually comes to mind is an expensive bump-out addition to the kitchen, or perhaps a complete bathroom make-over with all new fixtures, imported Italian marble tile and countertops, and a four-person hot tub. But a remodeling project doesn't need to involve a year of planning and a second mortgage to make a dramatic improvement to your home. Even the simplest, most inexpensive remodeling projects can have an instant payback in how well you and your family enjoy your home. And, in the process, it can increase the value of your house.

Replacing a worn-out window is a basic home remodeling project that can be accomplished in a single day, for only a small investment. But you'll get value from the investment every time you gaze out into your yard without recoiling from a cold draft or finding yourself staring at rotted wood and blistered paint.

Removing a partition wall can create a mess and may bring about a surprise or two—like re-routing a doorbell wire or spending the better part of a weekend trying to patch your ceiling. But the overall cost is low, and the time investment pales when compared to the open, airy feeling created in a space that used to be dreary and dark.

In *Home Remodeling: Walls, Windows & Doors,* you and other members of the Handyman Club of America will find information and ideas for a wide range of home remodeling projects. Follow along with the beautiful, full-color photographs, and witness the improvements as they unfold:

• A series of cramped, unfriendly rooms become an inviting, open living area when one wall is removed.

• A gracious bay window brings the beauty of nature into a quiet living room.

• An ordinary patio door transforms a drab basement and a dark three-season porch into bright, lively living spaces.

• In all, more than a dozen information-packed remodeling projects are presented in great detail.

Everyone who owns a home has a dream project—an island kitchen, a solarium, a second-floor addition with a master bedroom suite... But as much fun as it is to dream, sometimes you need to start a little smaller. In choosing the wall, window and door remodeling projects featured in this book, we had one basic goal in mind: to cover the home remodeling projects that *people actually do.* And as you stare up at the stars through your new skylight, or stand at the curb admiring your beautiful new entry door, who knows? You may find the inspiration you've needed to make that dream project finally happen. Or, you may discover that all it took was a new door or a better window or a well-placed wall to completely change the way you feel about your house.

Home Remodeling

Home remodeling is a sacred pursuit to most handymen. The home is where our skills, knowledge and energy are applied. And most of us have a wish list of home remodeling projects that's longer and more detailed than the mortgage applications we filled out before moving in.

Remodeling is an ongoing process, and the end never appears to be in sight. But for the true handyman, the endless nature of remodeling is a challenge that brings everchanging goals and lets us take our hobby in new directions. Each project we complete is an accomplishment in itself, and as the completed projects mount up we gain a special relationship with our homes that make them a source of comfort and pride.

In this book you'll find a wealth of information and ideas to help you get started with some of the most common projects that are probably at the top of your remodeling wish list—projects that involve walls, windows and doors. Although not always the most glamorous, these projects are the backbone of any home remodeling project.

Before

These before-and-after photos show quite dramatically the improvement you can make to your home with a single remodeling project. Replacing a small, unappealing entry door with a sliding patio door gave this room and three-season porch a new lease on life. This remodeling example teaches a good lesson: It doesn't always take a huge project to create big results.

Bring in the sunlight. Bay windows are popular for a number of reasons, but adding light to a room is at the top of just about every list. With the addition of the side sashes that project out from the house, the amount of glass is nearly doubled when an ordinary window is replaced with a bay window. And for the home's occupants, including the little fellow basking on the seat board, that means twice the warmth.

Accent your decor. The clean lines and rich color of this new interior door blend with the rest of the room to form a complete and highly appealing package.

Give the exterior side a lift. Although we focus mostly on the interior side of windows and doors (after all, we tend to see that face the most), a beautiful new window improves the outward appeal of a home as well. In the bay window above, the elegant multi-light panels and muntin grilles add charm and sophistication to a wall that would otherwise be plain siding and glass.

Create character. The beauty of windows and doors is that you can find (or build) one in just about any size and style. You wouldn't guess, from looking at them, that these multilight double-hung windows are new. But the custom casing and careful finishing downplay their state-of-the-art construction and make them natural focal points in the parlor area of this older home.

Add convenience plus style. This raised-panel double pocket door proves that you don't have to give up good looks in favor of function.

Skylights or roof windows, whichever name you prefer, fill this kitchen with luxurious natural light.

A room with a view. A casement-style picture window brings this glorious panoramic view right into the room.

Privacy you'll appreciate. Doors aren't only passageways; they can also be barriers. While blending perfectly with the decor in this home office, a slab-style door sends a subtle "Please don't disturb" message when closed.

Build a wall of glass.
Remodeling with walls, windows and doors can be quick and simple or elaborate and ambitious. These twin multi-light patio doors definitely fall into the second category. While your goals may be more modest, this project shows clearly that there's no limit to what you can accomplish with windows and doors.

Curb appeal, curb appeal, curb appeal. After location, curb appeal is one of the most important factors in selling a home. And virtually nothing does more to boost curb appeal than a striking entry door like the one shown here.

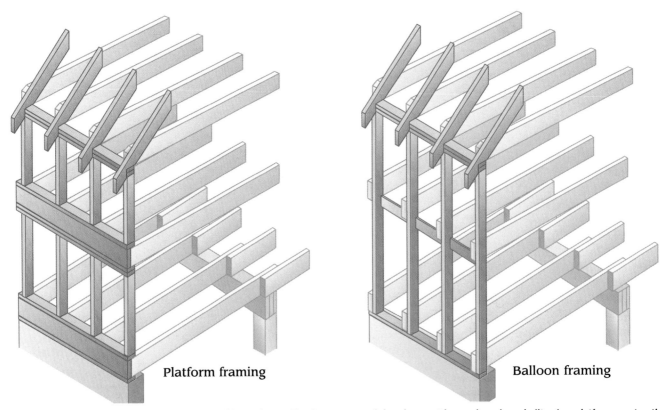

Platform framing   Balloon framing

Identify the type of framing system used to build your house. For the past several decades most homes have been built using *platform* construction (left illustration), where the stories of the house are essentially boxes stacked on top of one another. Some older homes rely on *balloon framing* as a construction method. Balloon-framed houses have exterior wall studs that rest on the sill of the house and run all the way to the rafters. The floor and ceiling joists are tied directly to the wall studs. Knowing which type of framing you have is important when you need to erect temporary supports and cut load-bearing wall studs. Because the vast majority of houses in America today use platform framing, the projects in this book all were completed on platform-framed houses, and the temporary support methods shown on the following pages are suitable only for platform-framed structures. If your home has balloon framing, consult with your building inspector for advice on providing temporary support.

Remodeling Basics

Replacing windows or doors and removing or building an interior wall are projects that often require you to make changes to the basic structure of your house. It's critical that you understand how any remodeling project will affect the structure of your house, and that you proceed with a plan that doesn't jeopardize that structure.

The first step in any remodeling project should be to study your house. This is true for reasons of design and decorating as well as structural integrity. Determine if your house is built using platform or balloon framing (See above). Identify which walls are load-bearing (See page 44). And involve your local building department from the outset. It's helpful to think of your building inspectors as partners in your project. And you'll usually find that they're more than happy to help, especially on complicated span and load-bearing issues. If your project will affect the mechanical systems in your house (wiring, plumbing or heating), you'll also want to consult with your building department for advice (and, of course, for building permits when required).

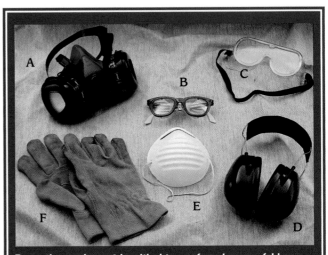

Protective equipment is critical to a safe and successful home remodeling project. Wear a respirator (A) whenever working with dangerous chemicals or very fine dust; safety glasses (B) or goggles (C) shield your eyes whenever operating power tools or performing any potentially dangerous activity—even striking a nail with a hammer; wear hearing protection (D) when operating power tools; a particle mask (E) prevents you from breathing in dust; and work gloves (F) should be worn whenever handling building materials.

TEMPORARY SUPPORT METHODS

Install temporary support from below whenever cutting load-bearing wall studs. The two methods shown at right both accomplish the same objective: to prevent the ceiling joists from sagging when the studs that support them are removed. Temporary support should be provided no more than 3 ft. from the framing members being removed. The beam, usually a doubled or tripled 2 × 4 or 2 × 6, should extend at least 2 to 3 ft. beyond the area where the studs are being removed. Make sure the temporary support is arranged so the beam is perpendicular to the ceiling joists, and leave the temporary support in place until the permanent support (a new header or beam) is installed.

Screw posts and beam

Temporary stud wall

HEADERS & BEAMS

A

B

C

D

Headers and beams provide permanent replacement support when wall studs are removed in a remodeling project. A header is installed above a window or door opening (A). In most cases, the header can be made from standard dimension lumber doubled together face to face. Because the combined thickness of two pieces of 2× lumber is less than the width of a 2 × 4 stud, a strip of ½-in. or ⅜-in. plywood is usually sand-wiched between the boards (B). The required header size depends mostly on the width of the opening. A beam is installed to replace a wall (C), and usually it protrudes below the ceiling. Because they bear heavier loads, engineered beams (D) often are used. Always check with your building inspector to determine the exact beam support your project requires. Don't rely solely on general span charts.

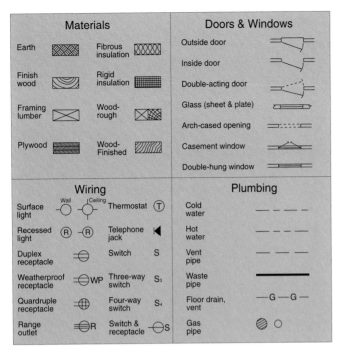

Materials				Doors & Windows	
Earth		Fibrous insulation		Outside door	
Finish wood		Rigid insulation		Inside door	
Framing lumber		Wood-rough		Double-acting door	
Plywood		Wood-Finished		Glass (sheet & plate)	
				Arch-cased opening	
				Casement window	
				Double-hung window	

Wiring					Plumbing	
Surface light	Wall / Ceiling	Thermostat	T	Cold water	
Recessed light	R / R	Telephone jack		Hot water	
Duplex receptacle		Switch	S	Vent pipe	
Weatherproof receptacle	WP	Three-way switch	S₃	Waste pipe	
Quardruple receptacle		Four-way switch	S₄	Floor drain, vent	—G—G—
Range outlet	R	Switch & receptacle	S	Gas pipe	

The chart above shows the standard symbols likely to be used when making a plan drawing for a remodeling project. Make careful plan drawings of your project. Not only are drawings required to obtain a building permit, they're also essential to conducting your project in an efficient and safe manner. For projects that involve removing or adding walls, start with a floor plan (below) that shows the scale of the project, any walls, windows or doors in the project area, and any mechanical systems present. For all projects, draw an elevation that shows the wall framing in the project area, as well as mechanical systems.

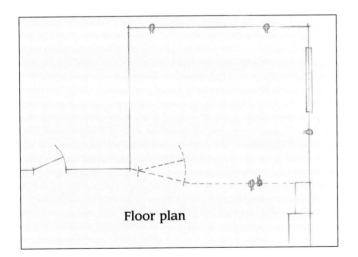

Floor plan

Planning checklist

❏ **Study your house.** Identify the type and location of framing systems and members; identify load-bearing walls; investigate and map mechanical systems (wiring, plumbing, ductwork) in the project area.

❏ **Research ideas.** Look through magazines, books, catalogs and other sources to learn about your options. Do some rough sketching and dreaming. Drive around your area to see what others with similar homes have done to increase window and door curb appeal.

❏ **Make a rough plan.** When you have a rough idea in mind, consider consulting with a designer, architect or reputable builder for their opinion. Meet with your local building inspector to see if your ideas are realistic for your home before you invest more of your time or money.

❏ **Finalize your plan.** Plans should include drawings, specific lists of materials needed, costs, probable time frame, and they should note points where help is needed, both from contractors and from friends, family or neighbors. If working with a contractor, be sure to have a signed agreement well before the start of the project.

❏ **Get a permit.** Submit your plan drawings and cost estimates to your local building department, along with permit applications. Don't expect an immediate answer.

❏ **Arrange for deliveries.** Once your plan is approved, break larger projects into stages and set a schedule. Arrange for delivery, if needed, and be sure you have a clear area to store building materials. Don't forget to arrange for waste disposal in projects that involve demolition.

❏ **Arrange for inspections.** Most projects that require a permit also will require on-site inspection at one or more stages of the project. Find out from your inspector when he needs to inspect the process, and schedule him early. Be realistic in your scheduling, and be prepared to make adjustments or changes.

Planning your project

Even with small-scale remodeling projects, planning is as important to success as doing the work. This is particularly true of projects that require a building permit. Generally, any project that involves structural modifications to your home, or electrical or plumbing work, will require a permit. Projects that cost in excess of $1000 or so usually require a permit, although the amount varies widely from area to area.

Planning is also important when working with contractors and for arranging follow-up inspections. As helpful as building inspectors can be, they have their own schedules to keep, and you shouldn't count on instant approval the moment you telephone or stop by the building department.

But most of all, careful planning ensures that the job will be completed correctly, on time and at the lowest possible cost to you.

Building tools for construction and installation include: circular saw with cross-cutting blade (A); drill/driver (B); staple gun (C); 4-ft. carpenter's level (D); jig saw (E); hammer drill for masonry (F); marking tools (G); sliding T-bevel (H); framing hammer (I); tape measure (J); carpenter's framing square (K); coping saw (L); plumb bob (M); chalk line (N); wood chisels (O); speed square (P). Additional power tools you may need include a power miter saw, a table saw and a router.

Demolition tools for removing walls, windows and doors and preparing for new wall openings include: circular saw with remodeler's blade (A); reciprocating saw with remodeler's or bi-metal blade (B); maul (C); flat prybar (D); "cat's paw" prybar and nail puller (E); and nippers for cutting nails and screws (F).

Tools & Materials

Selecting the best windows and doors for your remodeling project is one key to success, but without the right demolition and installation tools and building materials, your project will be a struggle. With each project shown in this book, you'll find a list of tools and materials you'll need to complete the project. Examples of most of the tools and materials are shown on the following pages and throughout this book. Use this list as a starting point, keeping in mind that your actual needs may vary based on your specific situation, the product you're installing and your own work habits. But whichever tools and materials you need for your project, bear in mind that keeping your tools in good working order and fitting them with the right blades, bits and accessories will ensure that they work properly for you. And when purchasing new tools and materials, don't cut corners. It would be a shame for a $500 window to fail because you bought the $2 caulk cartridge instead of the better $4 product.

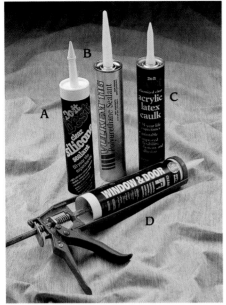

Caulks, adhesives and glues you'll likely need for remodeling projects include: (left photo) clear silicone caulk (A); high-grade polymerized exterior sealant (B); all-purpose caulk (C); paintable caulk (D); (middle photo) wallboard adhesive (E); decking/subfloor adhesive (F); general-purpose construction adhesive (G); contact cement (H); (right photo) two-part epoxy glue (I); yellow carpenter's glue (J); white household glue (K); hot glue gun (L).

Insulation for home remodeling projects includes: kraft-faced fiberglass batts for exterior walls (A); unfaced fiberglass batts for filling exterior-wall gaps (B); expandable foam insulation for small gaps (C); insulation sleeves with loose fiberglass for working in small, enclosed areas (D).

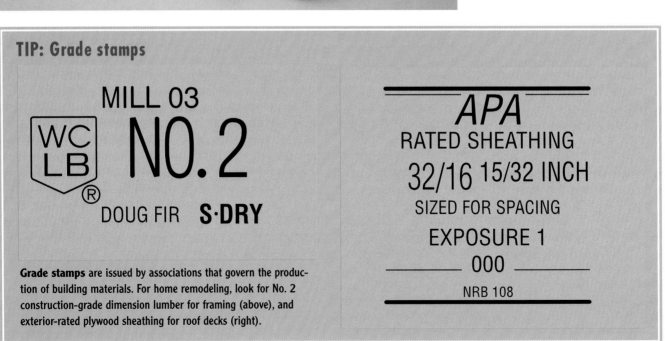

TIP: Grade stamps

MILL 03
WC LB ®
NO. 2
DOUG FIR **S·DRY**

APA
RATED SHEATHING
32/16 15/32 INCH
SIZED FOR SPACING
EXPOSURE 1
000
NRB 108

Grade stamps are issued by associations that govern the production of building materials. For home remodeling, look for No. 2 construction-grade dimension lumber for framing (above), and exterior-rated plywood sheathing for roof decks (right).

NAIL TYPES

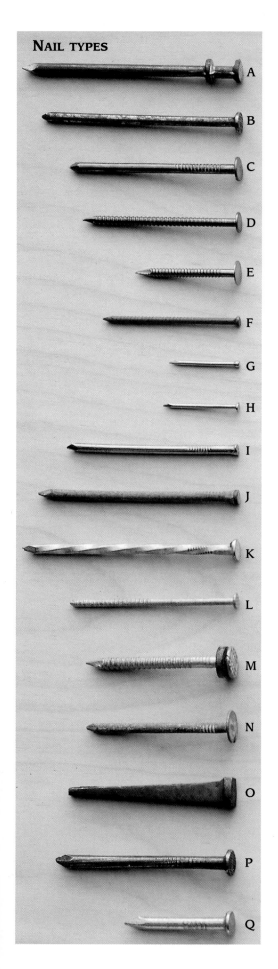

A
B
C
D
E
F
G
H
I
J
K
L
M
N
O
P
Q

NAIL SIZES

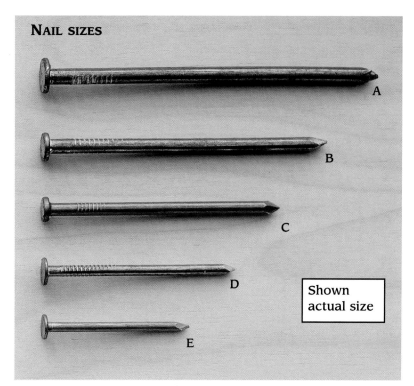

A
B
C
D
E

Shown actual size

Common nail sizes (above) include: 16d (A); 10d (B); 8d (C); 6d (D); 4d (E).

Nails types (left) for remodeling include: duplex nails (A); coated sinkers (B); common (box) nails (C); underlayment nails (D); wallboard nails (E); painted paneling nails (F); brads (G); wire nails (H); casing (finish) nails (I); galvanized casing (finish) nails (J); spiral (twist) nails (K); aluminum siding nails (L); rubber-gasket roofing nails (M); plain roofing nails (N); cut masonry nails (O); concrete (mortar) nails (P); joist hanger nails (Q).

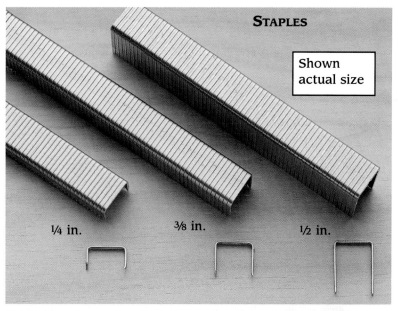

STAPLES

Shown actual size

¼ in.   ⅜ in.   ½ in.

Staples (above) are used mostly for attaching insulation and building paper in home remodeling projects. They're also used for temporarily attaching drop cloths and protective plastic sheeting. Use shorter staples for temporary tacking and longer ones for permanent fastening.

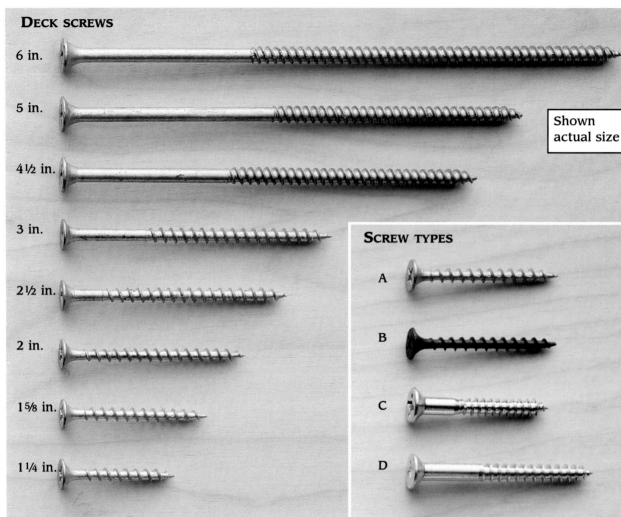

DECK SCREWS

6 in.

5 in.

4½ in.

3 in.

2½ in.

2 in.

1⅝ in.

1¼ in.

Shown
actual size

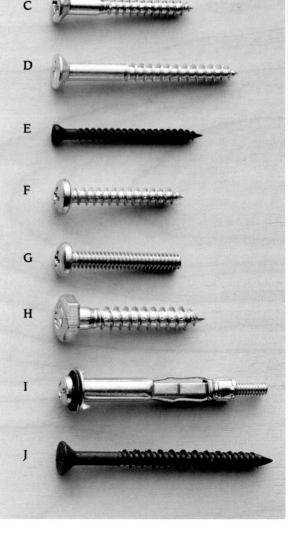

SCREW TYPES

A

B

C

D

E

F

G

H

I

J

Deck screws (above) are well-suited for exterior applications. And because they have widely-spaced threads, they hold well in softer framing lumbers. The thickness of the screws is uniform, but lengths vary from 1¼ to 6 in.

Screw types (right) vary in shape and style according to specific applications. Those likely to be used in home remodeling include: deck screws (A); wallboard screws (B); wood screws (C); brass-plated wood screws (D); trim head screws (E); sheet metal screws (F); machine screws (G); lag screws (H); wall anchors (I); high-low thread screws (J).

WOOD SCREW SIZES

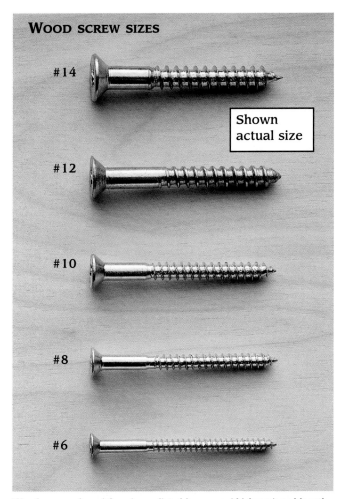

#14

Shown actual size

#12

#10

#8

#6

Wood screw sizes (above): are listed by gauge (thickness) and length. Gauge is expressed by a "#" symbol, and length is expressed in inches.

SCREW HEAD TYPES

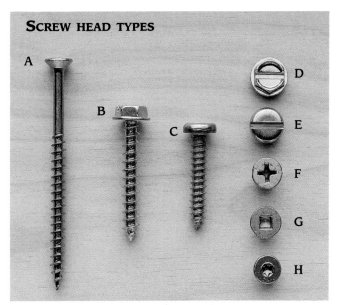

A

B

C

D

E

F

G

H

Screw head types vary by screw slot style and by head shape. Head shapes used in home remodeling include: flat head (A); hex head (B); pan head (C). Slot styles include: hex/slot (D); straight slot (E); Phillips head (F); square-drive (G); and torx (H).

BOLT SIZES

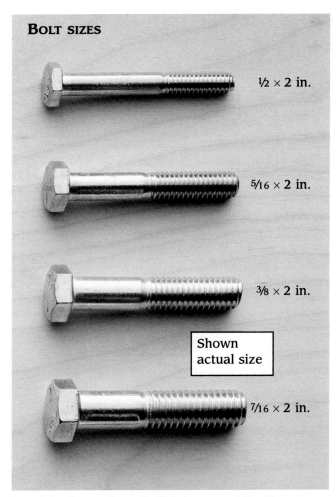

½ × 2 in.

⁵⁄₁₆ × 2 in.

³⁄₈ × 2 in.

Shown actual size

⁷⁄₁₆ × 2 in.

Bolts (above) are used occasionally in home remodeling. The most common are hex-head bolts that range in diameter from ¼ to ¾ in., and generally are available in ½- to 6-in. lengths

BOLT STYLES, NUTS & WASHERS

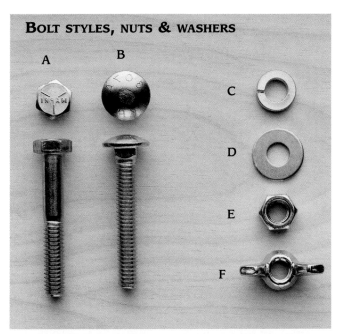

A

B

C

D

E

F

Bolt styles for home remodeling include: hex-head bolts (A) and carriage bolts (B); they're secured with either a lock washer (C) or a flat washer (D), and a standard hex nut (E) or wing nut (F).

Moldings & Trim

Installing moldings and trim can be a project all its own. In fact, adding decorative crown moldings, chair rail and other architectural details to a room can dramatically enhance the warmth and charm of the space.

Any wall, window or door project will involve some trim and molding work. It may be as simple as reattaching the original case molding around the frame of a new door or window. Or it may be as complex as custom-cutting trim pieces to help create transitions between a new window or door and the rest of the room. Whether simple or complex, the key to working with trim and molding is accuracy and care. Cutting mitered corners, even at a basic 45° angle, takes patience and precise setup of your miter box. Installing the trim pieces must be done using the correct methods and fasteners.

One of the trickiest aspects of trimming out a new window, door or wall is finding molding that matches the rest of the trim in your house. Not only should you find the same profile, but it should be made from the same type of wood and have a similar finish. If you can't find the perfect moldings at the lumberyard or building center, check millwork catalogs or salvage yards. If you still can't locate the right product, you'll either need to have it custom-made or make it yourself.

Installing molding and trim is the final step in most window or door installation projects. Case molding, shown during installation above, is used to frame most doors and windows today. It's mitered at the top corners and attaches to the front edges of the door jambs, leaving a slight reveal on the jamb.

Case molding trim kits are available in a variety of sizes, styles and wood types to fit most standard doors. The top two corners are pre-mitered for easy assembly. In most cases, the bottoms of the two long side jamb pieces will need to be cut to length before they can be attached to the door jamb.

TIP: Make your own moldings

Save money on molding by making your own using a profiling bit and a router or router table. Piloted router bits, like the double Roman ogee bit shown here, can cut a clean, decorative edge on just about any wood stock you'd consider using in your home. The cost of raw lumber is usually about ⅓ the cost of premilled moldings from the same material.

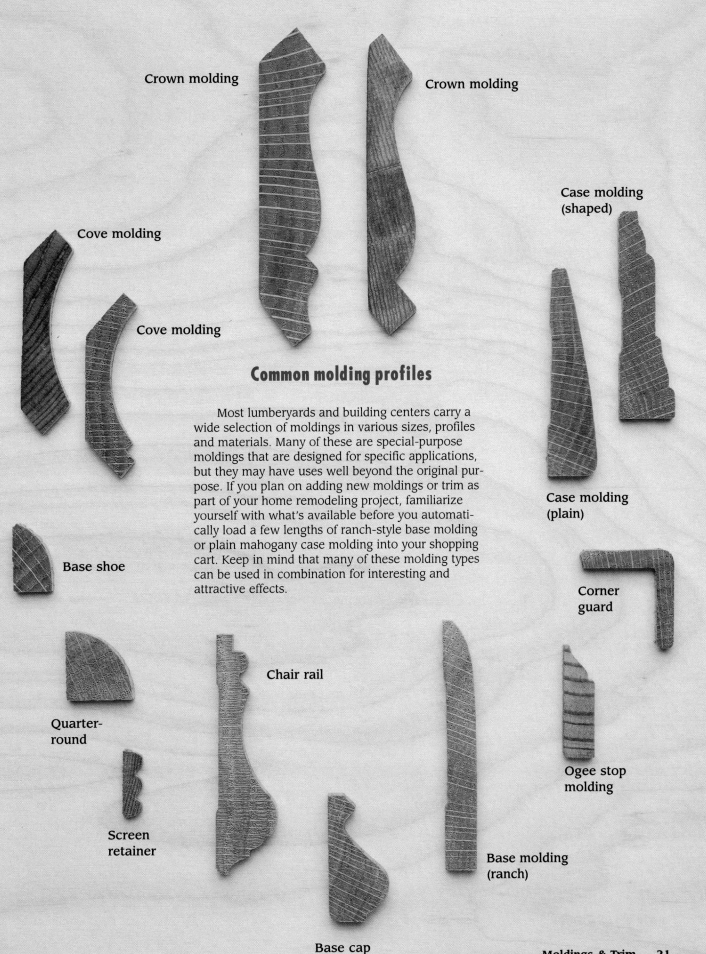

Crown molding

Crown molding

Cove molding

Cove molding

Case molding
(shaped)

Common molding profiles

Most lumberyards and building centers carry a wide selection of moldings in various sizes, profiles and materials. Many of these are special-purpose moldings that are designed for specific applications, but they may have uses well beyond the original purpose. If you plan on adding new moldings or trim as part of your home remodeling project, familiarize yourself with what's available before you automatically load a few lengths of ranch-style base molding or plain mahogany case molding into your shopping cart. Keep in mind that many of these molding types can be used in combination for interesting and attractive effects.

Case molding
(plain)

Base shoe

Corner
guard

Quarter-
round

Chair rail

Ogee stop
molding

Screen
retainer

Base molding
(ranch)

Base cap

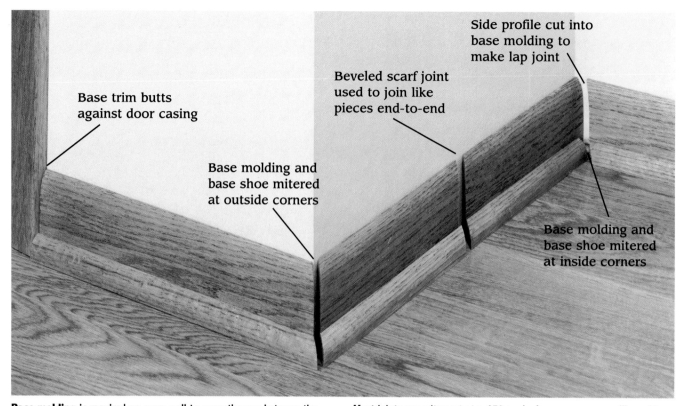

Base trim butts against door casing

Base molding and base shoe mitered at outside corners

Beveled scarf joint used to join like pieces end-to-end

Side profile cut into base molding to make lap joint

Base molding and base shoe mitered at inside corners

Base molding is required on every wall to cover the gap between the floor and the wall. It can be as simple as plain ranch molding, or you can dress it up a bit by combining different molding styles (See below).

Most joints are miter-cut at a 45° angle. In some cases, you'll need to cut the side profile of one adjoining piece so it fits around and against the other, as in the inside corner shown above.

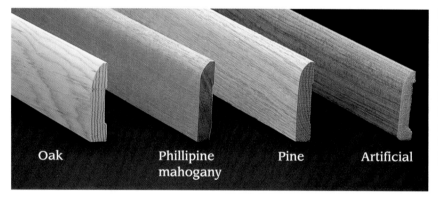

Oak

Phillipine mahogany

Pine

Artificial

Common wood types used for moldings include oak, Phillipine mahogany and pine. Recently, manufacturers introduced paintable moldings made from reconstituted wood and other products. While inexpensive and suitable for some applications, artificial moldings are not as durable as genuine wood products. TIP: When trying to match wood tones with the rest of the trim in your home, dab a little water on the molding sample. The wet color will be close to the actual color when a clear topcoat is applied.

MOLDING COMBINATIONS FOR CREATING BASE TRIM

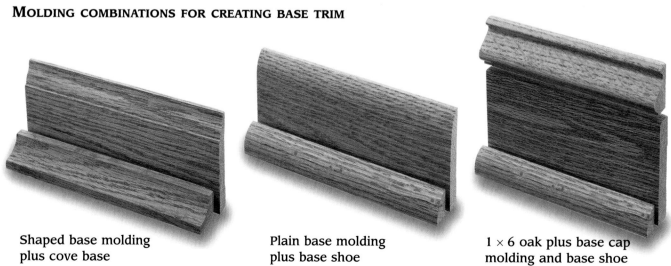

Shaped base molding plus cove base

Plain base molding plus base shoe

1 × 6 oak plus base cap molding and base shoe

1 It's a basic fact of trim carpentry that some profiled molding won't make clean miter joints at inside corners. Base molding is one of these types. To install base molding (ranch style is shown here), first attach one of the mating pieces so it butts up against the wall at the corner. Then, make a 45° bevel cut along the edge of the mating piece (make this cut before cutting the strip to finished length). *Tip: Apply finishing materials to molding pieces after cutting them, but before nailing them to the wall.*

2 Secure the molding with the top of the profile facing up and set a coping saw over the bevel edge so the blade of the saw is perpendicular to the back of the molding strip. Make a 90° cut, using the edge of the bevel cut as a cutting line. This will create an end that's square, but tapers upward to follow the molding profile. *Note: In some instances where walls do not meet at precisely 90°, you may need to trim away more material behind the profiled edge of the cope to achieve a tight fit between molding pieces.*

3 Apply finishing materials, then slip the trimmed molding piece into the corner so the overhanging profile follows the profile of the first molding piece. Attach with 4d finish nails. Drive all nail heads just below the surface of the wood with a nail set, then cover the nail heads with tinted wood putty.

Walls

When your house was built, it was probably with the expectation that the walls would stand unchanged for the life of the structure. But as your needs and desires change, removing or adding walls is a good way to use your remodeling skills to improve how well your home serves your family.

Most wall remodeling projects fall into two categories: adding a partition (non-loadbearing) wall, or removing an interior wall. Partition walls are added to divide a large room into two smaller, more private spaces or to finish an unfinished area of your home (usually a basement or attic). Walls are removed to create a more open feeling in the major living areas of a home or to annex one room to another to increase the floor space—for example, creating a master bedroom suite from two small bedrooms.

Any wall remodeling project requires carpentry, framing and finishing knowledge and skills. But most also will involve some wiring work: either removing or rerouting the old circuits, or installing new electrical and lighting. Walls also can contain plumbing or ductwork that may require relocation. Be sure to consider the potential impact of wiring, plumbing and ductwork when planning your wall project and when applying for building permits.

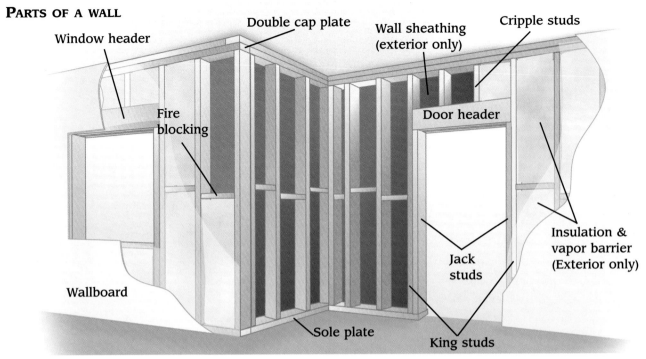

Window header
Double cap plate
Wall sheathing (exterior only)
Cripple studs
Fire blocking
Door header
Insulation & vapor barrier (Exterior only)
Jack studs
Wallboard
Sole plate
King studs

The basic parts of a wall are the framing members (sole plates, cap plates and wall studs) and the wall covering (wallboard, plaster or paneling for interior walls, sheathing and siding for exterior wall surfaces).

Exterior walls tend to contain more elements, including window and door framing and insulation. Interior walls are more likely to contain wiring or plumbing systems.

Wall Basics

Practically every remodeling project will involve walls in some facet. Adding or replacing windows and doors often requires that you make alterations to the wall framing. Creating a master bedroom suite may require that you remove or relocate a wall. Finishing off an unfinished basement usually means building several partition walls to divide the open area into finished, usable space. To understand fully what you're getting into with your remodeling project, start by learning the basics of wall construction.

Interior and exterior walls are similar in most ways. They're essentially an internal framework of vertical and horizontal framing members that support wall coverings, conceal wiring, plumbing and ductwork and contain openings for windows and doors. Exterior walls are generally thicker than interior walls and contain insulation, a vapor barrier and wall sheathing. Except when soundproofing is an issue, interior walls are hollow.

As a general rule, walls fall into two categories: loadbearing and non-loadbearing. In most homes built today, all exterior walls are loadbearing, and the majority of interior walls are non-loadbearing partition walls. Before removing or altering a wall, you should know for certain whether or not it is loadbearing (See page 44).

PROJECT 1: BUILDING A PARTITION WALL

PROJECT 2: REMOVING A WALL

An unfinished or partially finished basement is an excellent candidate for a partition wall. In the project shown above, an open and underused corner is converted into a private bedroom by erecting a partition wall.

Partition Walls

Partition walls are non-loadbearing walls erected to enclose a portion of a larger area and create more useful space with greater privacy. Partition walls are built most frequently in unfinished space (such as a basement) to make new rooms like a bedroom, bathroom, laundry room or home office. In some cases, you may want to add a new wall in a finished area to create a dedicated space for a special purpose. Common projects in finished space include dividing a large, informal living room into a formal dining room and a smaller living room. You can add a wall to create an intimate breakfast nook in a large kitchen or perhaps to separate visually an area near your entrance used as a mudroom or a laundry room.

Building a partition wall is a project that can easily be broken down into several phases and accomplished over a series of weekends. As with any remodeling project, you'll need to draw up a good plan and schedule for ordering materials and bringing in contractors if needed. In most cases, building a partition wall will require a permit. The actual construction of the wall may not require a permit, but any new electrical service or ductwork will need to be inspected and approved. And if the new wall will create a new room or decrease the size of any existing room, there are codes pertaining to minimum room size and emergency exits that you should be aware of. For example, if your partition walls will create a bedroom area in an unfinished basement, you'll need to make sure that you also create a secondary means of exiting in case there is a fire. A window large enough to allow passage to the outside (called an *egress* window) is typically used to meet this code requirement.

Wallboard T-squares are used to square and measure sheets of wallboard for cutting, and can be used as cutting guides.

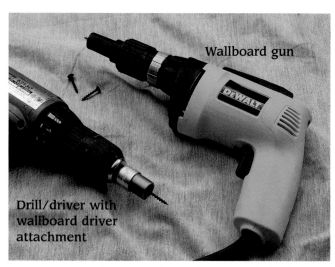

Wallboard guns and special attachments for your power drill keep you from overdriving wallboard screws.

Wallboard knives come in a variety of blade widths for spreading joint compound. Wallboard hawks are hand-held metal trays that make handling smaller quantities of joint compound easier.

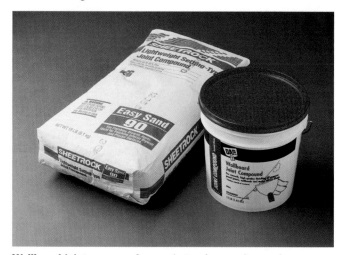

Wallboard joint compound comes in two forms—dry powder or premixed in one- or five-gallon pails.

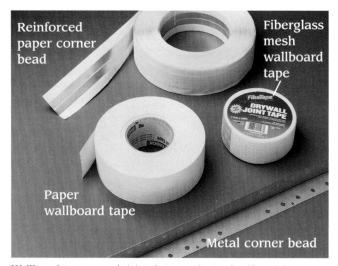

Wallboard tape conceals joints between sheets of wallboard. It comes in paper or fiberglass mesh forms. Corner bead is used to create inside or outside corners.

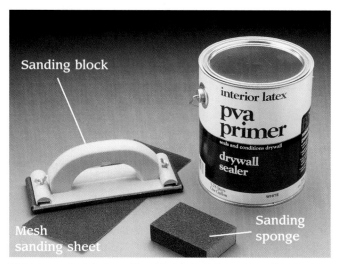

Finishing materials for wallboard joints include mesh sanding sheets and a sanding block, a sanding sponge for final sanding and wallboard sealant to apply before painting.

A detailed plan drawing is a necessity for obtaining a building permit and for successfully completing your wall remodeling project. The wall we'll build on the following pages is represented by dashed lines in the drawing to the right. The new wall and door separate a portion of the larger L-shaped common living area into a new bedroom. *NOTE: Basement living spaces must meet certain building code stipulations like escape routes, ceiling height and percentage of natural light available. Be sure to check with your local building inspector and have a permit approved before beginning a basement project like this. See page 14 for more information on plan drawings.*

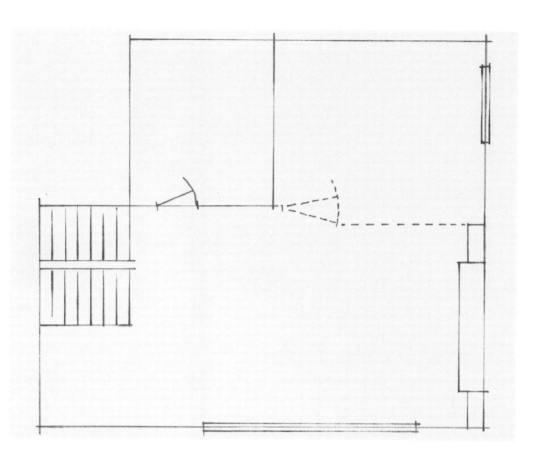

TIP: Hang wallboard on the horizontal

Minimize vertical seams by hanging wallboard horizontally whenever possible. Vertical seams are tougher to reach for taping and finishing, and you'll have more of them. One drawback to hanging wallboard horizontally is that end joints where wallboard sheets meet will not have a "channel" for joint compound. In these cases, feather successive layers of compound carefully so as not to mound the joints, which will require more sanding to mask them.

Building a partition wall

The best way to build a partition wall is to stick-build it in place. Some builders prefer to pre-build the wall frame then raise it into position. But for most remodeling projects, this method is ineffective. Stick-building a wall involves attaching the cap and sole plates to the ceiling and floor, then cutting individual wall studs to fit between the plates. The stud lengths can vary, but this method will ensure that the partition wall fits the space properly.

Tools you'll use:
- Circular saw
- Drill/driver
- Stud driver
- Hammer
- Level
- Keyhole saw
- Wallboard square
- Utility knife
- Chalk line
- Wallboard lifter

Materials list:
- Dimension lumber
- Wood shims
- Stud driver fasteners
- 10d nails or screws
- Construction adhesive
- Wallboard and wallboard finishing supplies

How to Build a Partition Wall

FIGURE A: Square the end sole plate to an adjoining wall. You can use a large carpenter's square, but the "3-4-5" triangularization technique being demonstrated above is usually more reliable. Step 1 outlines the method.

FIGURE B: Lay the sole plate members into position, marking key framing members and cutting angles as you go. When laying out corners, overlap the mating sole plate members and mark the intersection points (make sure to slip a spacer under the overlapping member). When marking non-right angles, as in the photo above, mark and cut the overlapping sole plate member, then reposition it and trace the edge to form a cutting line for the other member.

Before starting to build the wall, remove any base trim or other obstructions in the areas where the new wall will tie in to the existing walls and the ceiling and floor.

1 Begin by laying the sole plates in rough position on the floor, according to your building plan. Refine the layout by squaring the end sole plates to the walls they butt against. We used the "3-4-5 method" of squaring **(See FIGURE A)**. To use this method, first measure 3 ft. along the wall from the point where the end sole plate meets the wall, and mark a point on the wall. Then measure along the sole plate and mark a point 4 ft. away from the wall. Finally, secure the end of your tape measure at the 3-ft. mark on the wall and measure across to the end of the 4-ft. mark on the sole plate. Adjust the sole plate back and forth until the distance from the 4-ft. mark to the 3-ft. mark is exactly 5 ft. Mark the edges of the sole plate onto the floor for future reference.

2 Lay the remaining sole plates in position, using the squared sole plate as a point of reference. Mark cutting lines on the sole plate members at door openings, corners, end joints and any other angles or returns in the wall **(See FIGURE B).** Mark key wall framing members on the sole plates as you work. Cut the remaining sole plate members to fit and dry-assemble them together on the floor in finished position.

3 Trace the outlines of the sole plates onto the floor with a marker. If your floor has a floor covering, like carpet or sheet vinyl, remove the floor covering (but not the underlayment) inside the sole plate outlines **(See FIGURE C).** Be sure to leave the floor covering intact in door openings.

4 Fasten the sole plate members to the floor **(See FIGURE D).** Since the wall shown in this project is built on a basement concrete floor, we used construction adhesive and masonry nails to attach the sole plates to the floor. To drive the masonry nails, we employed a powder-actuated stud driver. If your wall is being built on a wood floor supported by floor

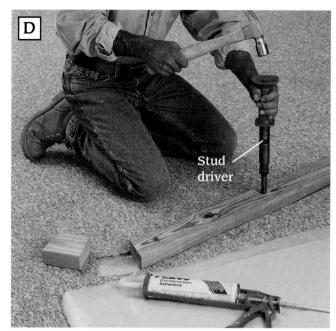

FIGURE C: Trace the outlines of the sole plate members onto the floor with a marker. Cut out and remove floor coverings in the outlined areas.

FIGURE D: Fasten the sole plate members to the floor. On poured concrete floors, use construction adhesive and masonry nails driven by a powder-actuated stud driver to secure the sole plate members.

Powder-actuated stud drivers employ gun powder charges to drive masonry nails through sole plate members and into concrete. Some stud drivers are trigger-activated (See above) and others discharge when the barrel end is rapped down against the sole plate (See FIGURE D). You can rent stud drivers at most rental stores. Always wear eye protection when using stud drivers.

FIGURE E: Cut a 2 × 4 equal in height to the distance from the tops of the sole plates to the ceiling. Set the 2 × 4 on the sole plates at regular intervals, level it and use it as a guide for drawing a mirror image of the sole plate layout onto the ceiling.

joists, mark joist locations on the subfloor and nail the sole plate members directly to the joists with 16d common nails. *TIP: Use pressure-treated lumber for sole plate members in basement or damp-prone applications.*

5 Mark the wall outline onto the ceiling, directly above the sole plate members. First, measure from the ceiling to the top of one of the sole plate members, then cut a 2 × 4 stud to that length. Set the stud on the sole plate at one end of the wall and use a level to adjust it until it is level and plumb. Mark the edges of the stud onto the ceiling, then shift the stud, adjust it to level and plumb and make additional outlines on the ceilings at intervals of 2 ft. or so **(See FIGURE E).** Mark all corners. Connect the reference points with chalklines to create a wall outline on the ceiling.

FIGURE F: If the partition wall runs parallel to the ceiling joists or crosses the joists at an angle, you'll need to install blocking in the joist cavities to create nailing surfaces for the cap plate members. Cut out a small section of the ceiling inside the cap plate outline to determine whether blocking will be needed. If the cap plates are parallel to the joists, use an electronic stud finder to locate the positions of all the joists in the project area, mark the joist locations, and attach the sole plate members by driving 3-in. wallboard or deck screws up through the cap plates and the ceiling covering and into the joists.

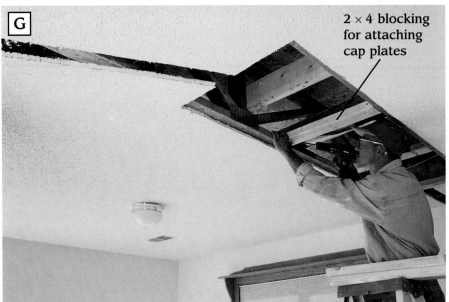

2 × 4 blocking for attaching cap plates

FIGURE G: To install 2 × 4 blocking in the joist cavities, you'll need to remove the ceiling covering concealing the cavities. Score the covering material with a utility knife, following the centerlines of the joists, then remove the material with a flat prybar. Cut 2 × 4 blocking pieces to fit the full width of the joist cavity, and attach them at 24-in. intervals with 2-in. wallboard or deck screws driven toe-nail style into the joists. The bottom face of each piece of blocking should be flush with the bottoms of the joists.

FIGURE H: Attach the cap plate members to the ceiling joists or blocking, using 3-in. wallboard or deck screws. If you've removed the ceiling covering, you'll need to redraw outlines for the cap plate locations using a leveled stud as a guide (See FIGURE E). Gang-mark framing member locations on the matching sole plate and cap plate members before installing the cap plates.

6 If you are unsure about the orientation and spacing of the ceiling joists, do a little investigating. Remove a small section of the ceiling covering **(See FIGURE F)**. Make sure the cutout is inside the outlines of the wall location. If the wall runs parallel to the joists or crosses them at an angle, you'll need to install 2 × 4 blocking between the joists to create nailers for the cap plate members. This will require you to remove additional sections of the ceiling covering so you can create access for installing the blocking.

7 Cut 2 × 4 blocking to fit between the ceiling joists above the cap plate location. Make sure you'll have a sturdy nailing point every 2 ft. along the wall outline. Attach the blocking with 2-in. deck screws **(See FIGURE G)**. The bottom faces of the blocking should be even with the bottoms of the ceiling joists. *NOTE: Also check to make sure there are framing members behind the wall surfaces at the points where the new partition wall will tie into existing walls. If not, you'll need to install blocking in the wall cavity in the same way shown for the ceiling blocking.*

8 Measure and cut 2 × 4 cap plate members that match the sole plate members. Do not cut out for door openings. Lay the cap plate sections next to their sole plate counterparts first and gang-mark wall stud locations at 16-in. intervals. Be sure to account for jack and king studs on each side of door openings. Attach the cap plates to the ceiling joists or blocking with 3-in.-long wallboard or deck screws **(See FIGURE H)**.

9 Begin installing the wall studs, starting at the ends of the wall. Measure for each stud individually and cut a 2 × 4 to fit. Apply construction adhesive to wall surfaces that will be attached to new wall studs. Set the new studs into position, adjust for level and plumb, then attach them to the sole plate and cap plate toenail style, using 3-in. deck screws **(See FIGURE I)**.

10 Install intermediate studs at the stud location outlines on the cap and sole plate reference marks **(See FIGURE J)**. They should be plumb and parallel.

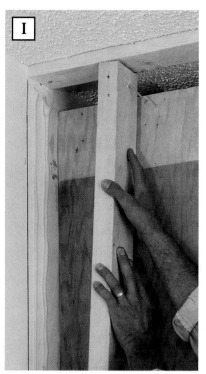

FIGURE I: Install the end corner studs first. Apply construction adhesive to form a bond with the abutting walls, then drive 3-in. wallboard or deck screws at 12-in. intervals.

Doorway location

FIGURE J: Attach intermediate studs and door framing members to the cap and sole plates, aligning each one over the plate reference marks.

FIGURE K: Attach door headers and cripple studs to complete the framing for doors. See pages 102 to 119 for more information on installing interior doors.

11 Frame the rough opening for the door with a header, cripple studs, king studs and jack studs **(See FIGURE K).** For more information on door framing, see pages 110 to 113.

12 Patch open areas in the ceiling with wallboard the same thickness as the ceiling covering. Before you begin installing wallcoverings, install (or have installed) any wiring, receptacles and switches, as well as any other internal wall elements, including ductwork and plumbing. IMPORTANT: **Have all wiring inspected and approved before you begin to install the wall coverings.**

TIP: If the wall you're building will enclose a bedroom near a common living area, consider soundproofing it by installing fiberglass insulation batts or acoustic tiles in the wall cavities before you attach the wallcoverings.

13 Make a detailed plan for installing your wallcoverings. Carefully measure the actual sizes of the walls, and plot out a layout for the wallboard pieces that makes efficient use of the materials and minimizes the number of seams. In most cases, hanging the wallboard in two horizontal rows will help to minimize the seams you'll need to tape (See *TIP,* page 29).

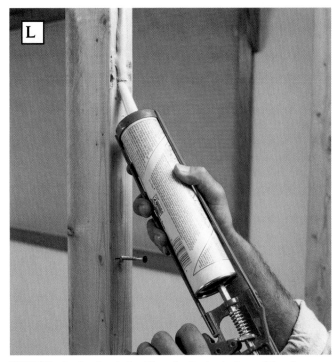

FIGURE L: Apply a bead of wallboard adhesive to the wall framing members before installing each piece of wallboard. Wallboard adhesive (you can get by with ordinary construction adhesive) strengthens the wall and helps deaden sound transfer through the wall.

14 Prepare to install the wallcoverings. Select a corner of the project area. If the wall is less than 8 ft. wide, cut the wallboard piece to length (See *Cutting wallboard,* right). If you're installing the wallboard horizontally, start with the upper row. To support the wallboard, drive a wallboard screw into each framing member just below a line where the bottom of the wallboard piece will fall. For reference, mark the midpoint of each wall framing member on the ceiling, near the wall (but far enough out that you can see the mark when the wallboard pieces are positioned).

15 Install the first piece of wallboard. With the piece cut to length and support screws driven into the framing members, apply a bead of wallboard adhesive to the wall framing members in the area where the wallboard piece will

Cutting wallboard

Step 1: Prop the wallboard sheet in a vertical position and score the finish surface along the cutting lines with a sharp utility knife. Use a wallboard T-square to ensure straight cuts. Anchor both ends of the straightedge when scoring to keep the straightedge from wandering during the cut.

Step 2: With the scored face of the wallboard facing away from you, snap the wallboard to break the gypsum along the cutting line. For full pieces, hold the wallboard on both sides of the cutting line and snap the piece in against your knee.

Step 3: Slice through the paper on the unfinished side of the wallboard, following the cutting line.

FIGURE M: Fasten the wallboard pieces to each framing member at intervals of 10 to 12 in., using 1¼-in. wallboard screws. Use a wallboard gun (shown here) or a drywall attachment chucked into your power drill. These tools prevent you from overdriving the wallboard screws and damaging the wall surface.

be attached **(See FIGURE L).** Set the wallboard piece on the temporary support screws (make sure you've got the finish face facing out). Position the piece so it butts tightly into the corner and is flush with the ceiling. Drive in a few wallboard screws to hold the piece in place. Using the stud location marks you made on the ceiling, snap chalklines onto the wallboard to indicate the centerline of each wall stud.

16 Fasten the wallboard piece to the wall framing members with 1¼-in. wallboard screws driven into each framing member at 10-in. intervals. The best tool for driving wallboard screws is the wallboard gun (See page 28), or you can use a wallboard screw attachment mounted in your regular drill/driver **(See FIGURE M).** Drive the screws so

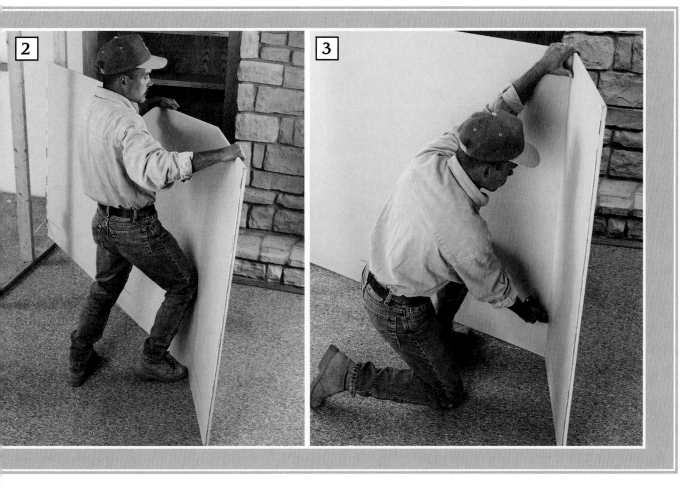

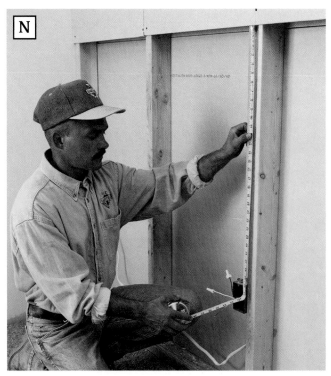

FIGURE N: Measure down to electrical boxes using the wallboard edge above it as a reference mark. Plot the location of the box onto the wallboard and draw an outline for cutting.

FIGURE O: Cut the opening in the wallboard for the electrical box, using a keyhole saw or wallboard saw.

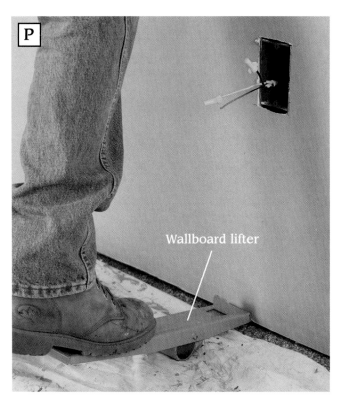

FIGURE P: Use a wallboard lifter to raise a piece of wallboard off the ground and flush against the piece above or the ceiling. There should be a gap of at least ¼ in. between the wallboard and the floor, especially in basement applications, to keep the wallboard from wicking up moisture from the floor.

the heads are just below the wallboard surface and a very slight recess (called a *dimple*) is created. The dimple is necessary for covering the screw head with joint compound. NOTE: *If you prefer, you can use wallboard nails instead of wallboard screws, but most installers use screws because they're faster to install, they hold better, and you aren't left with deep dimple marks in the wallboard resulting from the hammer blows.*

17 Install the rest of the upper row (in horizontal installations) on the wall. Leave a slight gap (no more than 1/16 in.) between wallboard pieces.

18 Begin installing the bottom row. To cut out for electrical boxes, first measure down to the top of the box from the bottom edge of the wallboard piece above it **(See FIGURE N).** Also measure in from the wall or wallboard edge that the piece will butt against. Transfer the measurements to the wallboard piece that will fit over the box, and outline the box in the correct position. NOTE: *There are many tricks floating around for marking cutouts on wallboard, including coating the edges of the box with lipstick and pressing the wallboard against it. Some of these tricks are effective, but as long as you're careful and don't confuse which side of the wallboard faces out, it's hard to go wrong by measuring.*

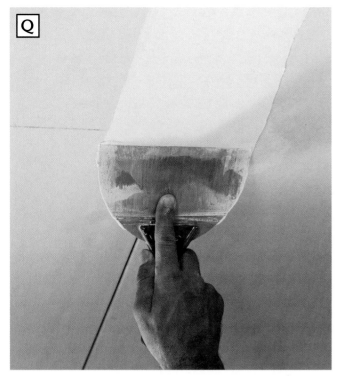

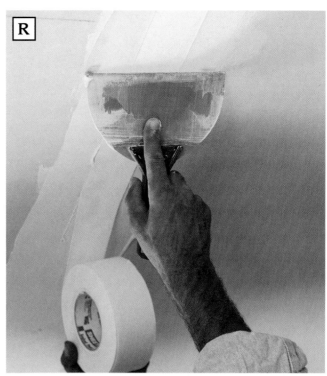

FIGURE Q: Cover wallboard seams and screw heads with joint compound applied with a 6-in. wallboard knife. When covering seams, work in small areas so you can bed wallboard tape into the joint compound before it dries.

FIGURE R: Press a strip of wallboard tape into the joint compound and smooth the joint with the wallboard knife. The compound should fill the factory-tapered edges of the wallboard.

19 Cut out the opening in the wallboard for the electrical box, using a wallboard saw or keyhole saw **(See FIGURE O).** Avoid tearing the paper facing as you cut—the switch plate or receptacle plate won't cover up as much as you might think.

20 Attach the wallboard pieces in the lower row. Use a wallboard lifter to raise the sheets off the floor and flush against the upper row **(See FIGURE P).** *TIP: A flat prybar supported by a 1 × 1-in. block of wood in a fulcrum position makes a convenient and effective wallboard lifter.* Install the remaining wallboard pieces.

21 Cover the screw heads or nail heads with joint compound, using a 6-in. wallboard knife. For conventional paper wallboard tape, use the wallboard knife to lay a bed of joint compound slightly wider than the tape over each wallboard seam **(See FIGURE Q).** If you're using fiberglass mesh wallboard tape with adhesive backing, apply the tape directly to the dry wallboard over the seams and press to create a bond.

22 Press strips of paper wallboard tape into the joint compound covering the seams **(See FIG-URE R).** Use the knife blade to cut the paper tape at the end of each run (See *TIP,* right). Run the blade of your wallboard knife gently over the tape to smooth

TIP: Cutting paper wallboard tape

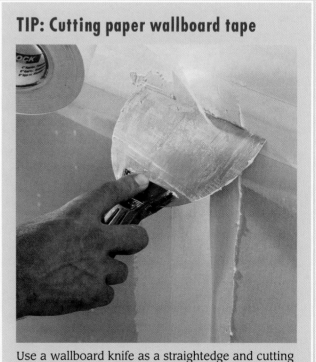

Use a wallboard knife as a straightedge and cutting instrument to cut paper wallboard tape. Press the knife blade firmly over the tape and against the wallboard, then pull the tape toward you and down at an angle to trim it.

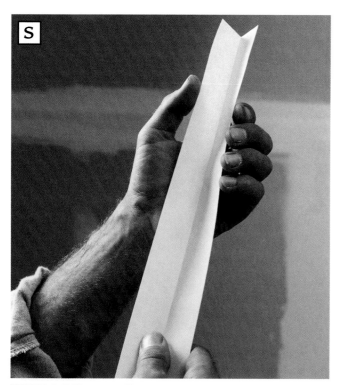

FIGURE S: Fold paper wallboard tape along the crease line before taping corners.

FIGURE T: Press the wallboard tape into beds of compound on each side of the corner.

Inside corner option: Reinforced paper tape

Paper wallboard tape reinforced with flexible metal strips is a good alternative to paper tape for finishing an inside corner. The metal strips keep the inside edge of the joint straight and even and help keep wallboard knives from wrinkling or damaging the tape. Fold it along the joint between the metal strips. The bare metal side of the tape should face the wallboard side of the joint (See left photo). Apply a first coat of joint compound to the wallboard on each side of the joint and press the tape into the compound, just as you do for paper tape. Smooth the edges of the joint and remove extra joint compound with a 6-in. wallboard knife (See right photo).

the joints and to squeeze out excess joint compound. It's very important that the surface of the tape remains recessed slightly from the adjoining surfaces of the wallboard. Enough joint compound should spill out from beneath the tape to fill the channels at the seams created by the factory-tapered edges of the wallboard. Carefully skim off any ridges in the joint compound. Let the joint compound dry.

23 At corners and at the joints between the wall and the ceiling, you can use ordinary wallboard tape to create a smooth edge, or you can use corner bead (See page 28) for an edge that offers greater protection (normally, metal corner bead is only used on outside corners). A third option is to use metal-reinforced paper tape, which offers the rigid, protective properties of metal corner bead but has a smooth paper covering that's easier to finish than the uneven surface of standard metal corner bead (See *TIP*, previous page). *If using paper tape,* crease the tape along the pre-folded crease line **(See FIGURE S)** and press it into a bed of joint compound to form the inside or outside corner **(See FIGURE T).** Run the knife blade over the tape to smooth it out, being careful not to slice through the tape at inside corners. The edges of the tape should be seated into and covered by joint compound. If the edges are not covered by joint compound, apply additional joint compound with your knife **(See FIGURE U).** Avoid overworking the joint. Too much smoothing can cause the tape to come loose or even to tear. *If using metal corner bead,* cut a strip of the bead material to cover the full height of the wall. Position the strip over the outside corner and drive a wallboard screw through the guide hole on one side at the bottom of the wall. Take care not to overdrive the screw—this can cause a kink in the corner bead. Press in gently on the edge of the corner bead to flatten it slightly. Don't flatten the bead so far that the ridge disappears. Drive a wallboard screw through the bottom guide hole on the other flange of the corner bead. The edge forms a ridge that helps contain the joint compound that will cover the corner bead and the screw heads. Work your way up toward the top, driving screws at intervals of 8 to 10 in. Take care to keep the protruding ridge as straight as possible. Apply joint compound over the flanges of the corner bead with a 6-in. wallboard knife. If the bead is very uneven, tape over the corner bead with folded paper wallboard tape, as described above.

24 After all seams are taped and all corner bead (paper or metal) is installed, allow the joint compound to dry completely. Then, apply a second coat of joint compound to each taped seam or corner, using an 8-in. wallboard knife **(See FIGURE V).** Feather the edges of the joint compound and knock down any ridges or high spots with your wallboard knife. Let the

FIGURE U: Smooth the edges of the tape on both faces of the corner, using your wallboard knife.

FIGURE V: Apply a second and third coat of joint compound over each taped seam, using an 8-in. wallboard knife, then a 12-in. knife. Feather these coats at the edges for a smooth transition between the joints and the the wallboard surface.

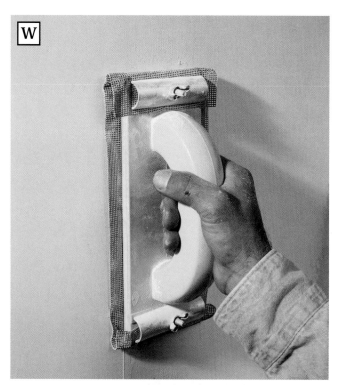

FIGURE W: Sand the dried joint compound until nearly even with the wallboard surface, using sanding mesh and a sanding block. Smooth out all irregularities in the joint compound, but be careful to not over-sand down to the tape.

compound dry completely. This coat is intended to fill and conceal the shrinkage at the edges of the tape.

25 Apply a third coat of joint compound with a 12-in. wallboard knife. Feather the edges, keeping the compound as even as possible. Let this coat dry. The surface, when dried, should be smooth, and it should project very slightly past the adjoining wallboard surfaces.

26 After all the joint compound has dried, sand the joints smooth. Use a sanding block with metal sanding mesh for the first stage, sanding until all ridges are knocked down and the seams are basically smooth and even. The sanding mesh works quickly, so take care not to be so aggressive that you sand all the way down to the tape—exposed tape will be rough when painted. If any tape shows through, reapply new compound **(See FIGURE W).** Wear a dust mask when sanding wallboard joints, and knock the dust loose from the mesh frequently. *TIP: If you are sanding a large area, you may want to use a mesh sanding block with a dust extraction port that hooks up to a vacuum cleaner hose.*

27 Wet-sand the joints and the spots covering the screw heads with a fine-grit sanding sponge

FIGURE X: Wet-sand wallboard joints with a sanding sponge and clean water to cut down on dust. The sponge should be damp but not dripping. Wring it out frequently to keep it from clogging with compound.

FIGURE Y: Apply wallboard sealant or latex wall primer to the new wall surface, using a paint roller.

dipped in clean water **(See FIGURE X).** The pad sponge should be damp but not dripping. The water helps keep fine dust to a minimum and cleans dry, loose dust from the surface. Before applying wallboard sealer or paint primer, wipe all seams with a slightly dampened rag.

28 Wallboard and joint compound are both very porous and should be treated with sealant before you apply wall paint. Roll on a coat of latex wallboard primer, or thick paint primer, to seal the wall **(See FIGURE Y).** After applying the sealant, examine the wall by looking down the length of the wall. If there are any rough areas or visible joints, apply another coat of wallboard compound, then sand and repaint the area when dry.

29 Paint the wall with latex interior wall paint. For a surface that looks as smooth and even as possible, use flat paint. For a painted surface that can be washed more easily (but calls more attention to any imperfections in the wall), use semi-gloss paint.

30 Install an interior prehung door in the door opening (See pages 103 to 108 for instructions on hanging a prehung door). Stain and topcoat matching door casing and base trim pieces, and attach them to the wall (See pages 107 to 108). Attach faceplates over electrical receptacles and switches.

FIGURE Z: Install the door in the rough opening. Then finish and fasten case molding and base molding to the walls.

Before

Removing a Wall

Remodeling your house isn't only about replacing outdated features or adding improvements. Sometimes, subtraction can yield better results than addition. Removing an interior wall is a good way to apply the "less is more" theory to home remodeling.

In older houses, the floor space usually was divided up by the architect or builder to create as many separate rooms as possible. A generation or two ago, 90 sq. ft. of floor space was considered adequate elbow-room for a bedroom. Today, 120 sq. ft. of open floor space is a bare minimum, and most bedrooms are 150 sq. ft. or larger, often featuring a spacious walk-in in closet as well. In the shared living areas, compartmentalization has also fallen out of favor. Where a typical old-house floor plan may feature a small kitchen, a pantry, a dining room, a parlor and a living room, today's home designs strive to eliminate

walls and even ceilings. Newer homes boast open floor plans, vaulted ceilings and a flexible approach to living space.

While *new* doesn't necessarily mean *better,* there are some good reasons that the shoebox approach to house design has become a thing of the past. From the turn of the century up to World War II, families and extended families were larger, and the average number of occupants sharing homes was greater. That meant that privacy was a critical design requirement.

Today, with smaller families and more leisure (and work) time being spent in the home, needs have changed. Bedrooms, for example, have been transformed from mere sleeping areas to multi-use rooms for sleeping, studying or working, exercising and even home entertainment. And as societal changes have greatly reduced the prominence of the older forms of interaction, like the dinner party, the need for formal dining rooms has diminished. Now, a large open kitchen with an eat-in area is the heart of the home. Dining rooms, when they exist at all, are usually closely connected to the living room.

Removing a wall is an easy way to update your older home and make it more desirable to today's home buyers. You can knock out a partition wall and convert two smaller bedrooms into a master bedroom with a walk-in closet and/or private bath. By removing a kitchen wall, you can annex an adjacent pantry or utility room to increase kitchen size (maybe adding that kitchen island or breakfast nook you've been talking about for years). Removing a wall between the living room and an under-used dining room gives you new options: perhaps buying a piano or beefing up your home entertainment system.

Before you begin dismantling walls and reconfiguring the floor plan of your home, consult with a designer or a remodeling professional so you can be sure your plan makes sense. Once you've started the wall removal process, it's difficult to turn back.

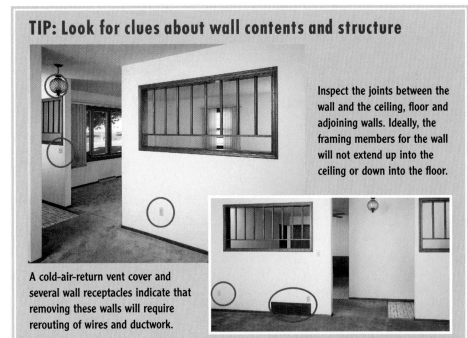

TIP: Look for clues about wall contents and structure

Inspect the joints between the wall and the ceiling, floor and adjoining walls. Ideally, the framing members for the wall will not extend up into the ceiling or down into the floor.

A cold-air-return vent cover and several wall receptacles indicate that removing these walls will require rerouting of wires and ductwork.

Look for signs of internal obstructions and clues to structural tie-ins when evaluating a wall that's a candidate for removal. Receptacle covers, switch plates, heating or cooling duct grilles and telephone jacks are obvious signs that the wall contains parts of your mechanical systems that will need to be rerouted. Also inspect the areas above and below the wall—if the wall is directly below a bathroom, for instance, it's likely to contain plumbing pipes. Peel back carpeting to see if the wall is built into the subfloor (which will require patching) and check the joints where the wall meets the ceiling and other walls to find out how framing members are connected.

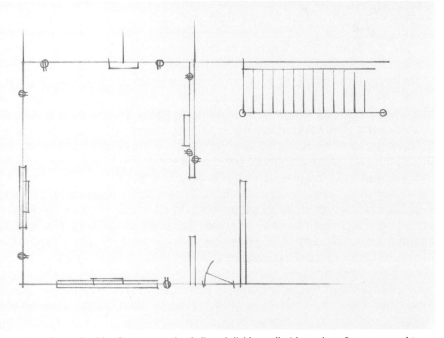

In the project shown in this chapter, a pair of aligned divider walls (shown in red) are removed to create an open living room and to visually integrate the new entry door with the rest of the house. An inspection of the attic space above the wall revealed that the walls supported the weight of the ceiling structure and thus needed to be treated as load-bearing walls.

Identifying load-bearing walls

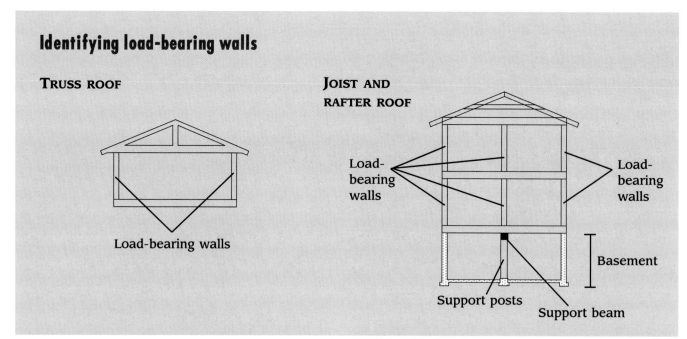

TRUSS ROOF

Load-bearing walls

JOIST AND RAFTER ROOF

Load-bearing walls

Load-bearing walls

Basement

Support posts

Support beam

Determining whether a wall is load-bearing takes a bit of detective work in the attic and basement. Examine your roof. If your home was built after 1950, it likely has a truss roof. Trusses are prefabricated "webs" made of 2-in. dimension lumber connected by metal brackets. Truss roofs transfer the weight of the roof down through the exterior walls and onto the foundation. Houses built before 1950 usually have joist-and-rafter roofs that are supported by a central wall on each floor of the house. The weight of each floor is transferred down this central wall system and through the exterior walls to the basement, where the central walls rest on a metal or wooden support beam and posts. If you are in doubt about the load-bearing structure of your roof and walls, have your home inspected before beginning any work that alters the structure of your walls.

Evaluating Walls

Before beginning wall removal, determine whether the wall is load-bearing or non-load-bearing. A bearing wall is so-called because it bears or supports the weight of the ceiling, floor or roof above it. A non-bearing wall is a partition or curtain that merely divides and defines the room but does not support any weight of the structure other than its own weight.

Removing a non-bearing wall involves dismantling the old wall and repairing the adjoining walls, ceiling and floor to conceal damage resulting from the removal.

To determine whether the wall you plan to remove is bearing or non-bearing, consider the basic construction of a house. In basements or crawl spaces you will find a center wall, or a wooden or steel support beam positioned at the center of the first floor. The floor joists meet at the center bearing member and are supported by it. A two-story house will have a central bearing wall on the first floor, extending the length of the house and located directly above the basement or crawlspace support beam or basement center bearing wall. The weight of the second floor is supported by this center wall.

Roof construction dictates whether a central wall in the main floor of a single-story house or the second floor of a two-story house is a bearing wall. If the roof is stick-built, or assembled on site from individual ceiling joists and roof rafters, the center wall is a load-

bearing wall and carries the weight of the roof. If truss construction was used to build the roof, the roof and truss system are supported by the exterior walls, and most of the interior walls are non-load bearing.

On any house, the exterior walls are load-bearing, and the load they bear should be supported by temporary walls or bracing during the demolition period. A beam or a header must be installed at any point where a new opening is cut into the walls.

If you are not sure whether a wall is a bearing wall, consult an inspector or a contractor before removing the wall. Structural damage may result if you remove a load-bearing wall without building temporary support to carry the weight of the structure that bears on it.

Removing a non-bearing wall

Removing a non-load bearing partition wall is a relatively simple task, at least from a structural standpoint. Neither temporary nor permanent support to replace the wall is required. But partition walls are likely to contain internal wall elements that will need to be rerouted if the wall is removed. Before removing any wall, inspect the wall to see if it conceals electrical wiring, plumbing or ductwork. If it does, or if you find any components unexpectedly after you've begun removing the wall, contact a licensed contractor to take care of the problem.

Preparing for wall demolition

Before beginning wall demolition, cover light fixtures, air conditioners and other room elements that should be protected from dust—trash bags are very handy for this purpose. Also cover air intake or heat vents with plastic sheeting (make sure the heating or cooling unit is turned off). Remove passage doors in the project wall. Tape plastic sheeting across doorways. In large rooms, make a wall of plastic sheeting to keep dust confined in as small an area as possible. Remove baseboard trim from the project wall. Open windows for good ventilation.

Removing a bearing wall & replacing it with a beam

Removing a load-bearing wall is a more complicated project than simply removing a non-load bearing partition wall. When removing a bearing wall you must install temporary support parallel to the existing wall to support the ceiling joists above the wall (See page 13 for temporary support options). This temporary support will carry the weight borne by the wall during the demolition process. When the demolition is done you must install a permanent support, usually a steel or wooden beam, to bear the weight. When the permanent support is in place you may dismantle the temporary support structure.

When considering a wall removal project, be aware that the beam required to replace a bearing wall almost always extends well past the ceiling surface and into the room below. In some cases, an intermediate support post is required to shore up the beam. If your intention is to create a large, seamless living area by removing a load-bearing wall, you'll likely be disappointed.

Tools you'll use:
- Reciprocating saw
- Circular saw
- Hammer
- Flat prybar
- Level
- Drill/driver
- Screwdriver
- Utility knife
- Metal support posts
- Stapler

Materials list:
- Plastic sheeting & tape
- Dimension lumber
- Wood shims
- 10d nails or screws
- Permanent support beam
- Construction adhesive
- Lag bolts & washers
- Wallboard for patching
- Wallboard screws

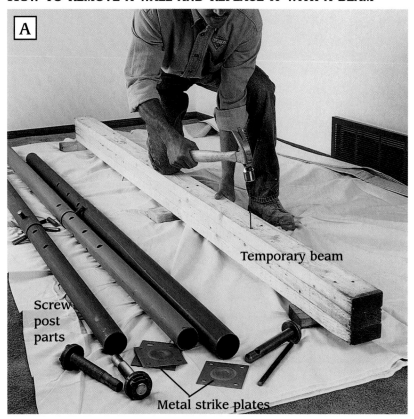

FIGURE A: Choose a temporary support method (See page 13) and assemble all the components you'll need. For this project, we used a temporary beam made from three 2 × 4s and supported by screw posts.

FIGURE B: Attach post strike plates to the beam at each post location. Bend back the nails for easier removal of the plate.

FIGURE C: Adjust the telescoping ends of the support posts so the beam is level and held securely against the ceiling. Adjust each post no more than ½ in. at a time.

1 After preparing the project site (See previous page), build a temporary support structure (See page 13). For the project shown here, we chose to use telescoping metal screw posts to support a temporary wooden beam. The screw posts rest on metal plates atop doubled 2 × 4s to distribute the weight. Assemble all the parts needed to build the temporary support wall **(See FIGURE A).**

2 Construct a temporary beam by face-nailing three 2 × 6s together. The beam should span at least 2 to 3 ft. beyond the removal area, if possible. If the span of the beam is greater than the length of the individual 2 × 6s, stagger the butt joints where the boards meet end-to-end so they're at least 2 ft. apart. The beam will be set in place with the edges of the 2 × 6s facing up.

3 Attach a heavy-duty metal strike plate to the beam at each post location

(See FIGURE B). Use enough posts so they're spaced no more than 6 ft. apart.

4 Raise the beam into position, about 2 ft. away from the wall. You may want to get a helper for this step. Install temporary 2 × 4 supports at each end of the beam to hold it against the ceiling while you install the screw posts. Adjust the posts to the approximate height needed, and set them in place so the tops will strike the strike plates and the bottoms are resting on a doubled 2 × 4 aligned with the beam.

5 Adjust the telescoping ends of the posts so they press the beam securely against the ceiling **(See FIGURE C).** Check with a level to make sure the beam is level. Do not overtighten the post adjustment—this can create several problems, including raising the ceiling joists and cracking the ceiling.

6 Shut off electrical service to the wall and surrounding areas at the main service panel. Never cut into a wall with live electrical service.

7 If the wall is clad with wallboard, use a sharp utility knife to cut through the wallboard tape at the corners between the wall and ceiling and the adjoining walls **(See FIGURE D).** This will minimize damage to wallboard on surfaces adjacent to the wall being removed. If the wall is plastered, use a hammer and a sharp mason's chisel to cut through the plaster at the corners where the wall meets adjacent walls and the ceiling. This also will minimize the damage caused by the wall removal and limit the extent of future repairs.

8 Use a flat prybar to remove the wallboard or plaster. When you have opened a small hole in the wallboard you will be able to grasp the edges of the wallboard and pull it away from the studs **(See FIGURE E).** This will limit dust to a minimum and reduce cleanup chores. If the plaster wall is older and deteriorated, or is backed by wood lath, you may be able to pull or pry away large chunks of plaster. Remove the largest chunks possible. The less breakage you do to the plas-

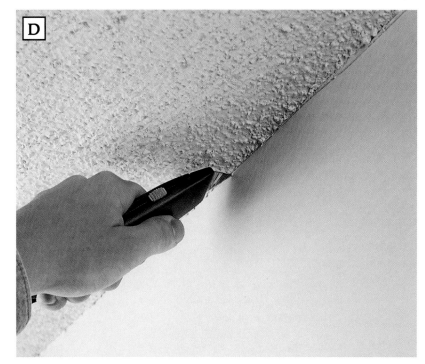

FIGURE D: Score along the joint between the wall and the ceiling with a utility knife. Also score the joints between the wall and the abutting wall or walls. This minimizes damage to the wall and ceiling coverings you're not planning to remove.

FIGURE E: Carefully remove the wall coverings with a flat prybar and by pulling away chunks. Always shut off electrical service at the main service panel before opening or cutting into any wall.

ter or wallboard during removal, the less debris and dust you will create. If the plaster is solid or is backed by rock lath (small panels similar to wallboard), prying it away will be a more difficult chore. You will have to use the prybar or ripping tool and pull the plaster away in small pieces.

FIGURE F: Remove wiring, plumbing and ductwork from the wall and reroute it. Unless you're an expert in these areas, hire a contractor for this part of the project.

FIGURE G: Begin removing wall framing members. Because the wall being removed here contained a passthrough framed with cripple studs that require no cutting prior to removal, we started work in this area.

9 When you have removed the covering from one side of the wall you can disconnect or reroute the wiring. **Unless you have extensive experience working with wiring, hire a licensed contractor to remove and reroute wiring.** Make sure the electrical service has been shut off at the main panel, and always check receptacles and switches with a neon circuit tester to make sure there is no live electrical current. Disconnect wiring at the nearest junction box outside the wall area, and remove the wires, conduit and boxes in the wall **(See FIGURE F).** Also remove any other wall elements, such as plumbing, ductwork or telephone cables. Hire appropriate contractors for these tasks as well.

10 With the internal elements all removed, strip the wall covering from the other side of the wall, then begin dismantling the wall framing members. If the wall you're removing contains a passthrough or doorway, start removing studs at these points **(See FIGURE G).** Cut full-height studs in half with a recip-

rocating saw and remove them by prying and pulling the cut ends free from the cap plate and sole plate **(See FIGURE H).**

11 Remove the corner studs where the wall meets adjoining walls. Use a flat prybar to pry the corners studs loose. Dispose of all removed framing members immediately.

12 Next, determine if you need to remove the 2 × 4 cap plate members. This is not always a black-and-white decision. The presence of the cap plate does not generally affect the required width of the beam you'll need to install to replace the wall, but it does cut into the available floor-to-ceiling height. For this reason, most remodelers will remove the cap plates and install the permanent beam flush against the bottoms of the ceiling joists whenever possible. In the project shown here, we chose to remove only the lower cap plate members and leave the upper cap plate members intact. Because the wall being removed

here only supports the weight of the ceiling materials in the living area, a relatively modest beam that doesn't project too far into the room could be used. And removing the upper portions of the doubled cap plate would likely have caused significant damage to the adjoining ceiling. We used a flat prybar to remove the lower portion of the doubled cap plate **(See FIGURE I).** *NOTE: Depending upon how the cap plate ties into the framing of adjoining walls, you may have to cut through the cap plate on a line flush with the adjoining wall.*

13 Remove the sole plate members, using a prybar and hammer. This will leave a gap in the floor that will need to be patched (See page 52).

14 Construct support posts from doubled 2 × 4s joined with 10d nails, and nail them to the wall framing members at each end of the new beam span **(See FIGURE J).** To determine the required length of the posts, measure the distance from the bottom

FIGURE H: Cut through intermediate wall studs with a reciprocating saw, and pry the stud sections away from the sole and cap plates.

FIGURE I: Remove the cap plate or cap plates by prying with a flat prybar. To avoid damaging the surrounding ceiling, we removed only the lower of the two cap plates.

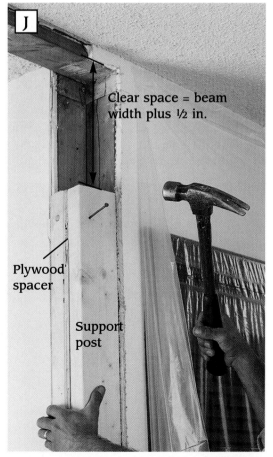

Clear space = beam width plus ½ in.

Plywood spacer

Support post

FIGURE J: Construct beam support posts and nail them to the framing members at the ends of the beam location.

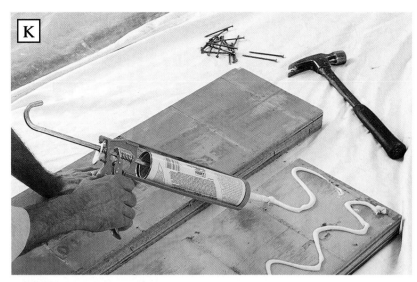

FIGURE K: Build the new support beam. Above, two engineered beams are bonded together with construction adhesive and 10d nails.

Screw post

FIGURE L: Use screw posts to force the beam up against the ceiling joists, then shim between the beam and the support posts to fill the gaps.

FIGURE M: Anchor the beam with lag bolts, if possible, and by driving deck screws toe-nail style through the beam and into adjoining framing members.

of the opening in the ceiling to the floor, then subtract the width of the beam plus ½ in. If necessary, add plywood spacers between the 2 × 4s so the outer face of the outer post is flush with the adjoining wall framing members (this will make it easier to install a wallboard patch).

15 Build the permanent beam **(See FIGURE K).** In the project shown here, we followed the recommendation of a local building inspector and used two engineered beams bonded together with construction adhesive and 10d nails. You'll be advised as to the size of the beam needed for your project when you apply for your building permit. See page 13 for more information on beam construction.

16 With helpers, raise the beam and set it into position on top of the end posts. Position a metal screw post near each end of the beam and raise the beam up until it fits snugly against the surface above it (an alternative to metal screw posts is to cut 2 × 4s a few inches longer than the distance from the beam to the floor, wedge the 2 × 4s between the beam and the floor, and drive the bottoms of the 2 × 4s toward the beam support posts, using a hammer or maul, to raise the beam). Drive wood shims between the post tops and the beam to level the beam and to fill space between the posts and the beam **(See FIGURE L).** Trim the ends of the shims flush with the support posts.

17 Anchor the beam to adjoining wall framing members with lag screws and washers **(See FIGURE M).** Drill counterbored guide holes for the lag screws. If the beam is not adjoined by any other framing members, attach it to the joists above and the posts below using 3-in. deck screws driven toe-nail style.

18 Fill in with loose fiberglass insulation around the support posts on any exterior walls, and staple a plastic vapor barrier to cover the exterior wall cavities **(See FIGURE N).** Add nailing strips as needed to patch wallboard around the openings in the wall cavities at each end of the beam.

19 Complete any rerouting of wiring or other wall elements before installing wallboard. Have the work inspected and approved before proceeding.

20 Depending on the type of beam you've installed, there are several options for finishing it. Most often, the beam is covered with wallboard and finished to blend in with the ceiling and walls. But on rustic homes, or if you've chosen to use a timber beam, you may want to give the beam an "exposed beam" look. With timbers, simply coat the beam with boiled linseed oil. Engineered beams and beams made from dimension lumber can be clad with strips of wood (cedar, redwood, oak, clear pine and fir are all good choices) then finished. Since the goal is to make the clad beam look like a solid timber, the best solution is to bevel cut the mating edges of the cladding to create a mitered box around the beam. For the project shown here, we simply cut strips of ⅜-in. wallboard to cover the exposed faces of the beam and attached them directly to the beam with 1¼-in. wallboard screws **(See FIGURE O).** We nailed strips of metal corner bead to the exposed corners for rigidity and protection **(See FIGURE P).** See pages 34 to 40 for more information on installing wallboard). Cut wallboard to create patches around the openings in the walls and attach with wallboard screws.

FIGURE N: Insulate openings in exterior walls and cover with a plastic vapor barrier before applying wallboard. Attach nailing strips for the wallboard before insulating.

FIGURE O: Cover the beam and all exposed wall and ceiling areas with wallboard patches.

FIGURE P: Nail metal corner bead with wallboard nails driven every 8 in. to protect new wallboard corners.

FIGURE Q: Scrape textured ceilings with a wallboard knife to prepare them for wallboard joint tape and compound.

FIGURE R: Apply joint compound to seams and corners, and press wallboard tape into the joint compound. Smooth with a wallboard knife.

TIP: Patch carpet with a carpet seamer

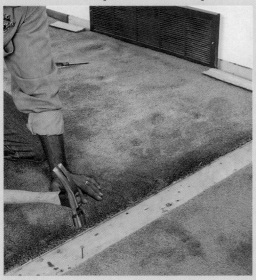

Because you've removed the sole plate, there will be a gap in the floor covering and perhaps the subfloor. To patch gaps in carpeted floors, first nail filler strips so the floor in the patch area is even with the surrounding floor underlayment. Find carpet pad and carpet that match the existing carpet (the first place to look is in closets and other lightly-used areas of the house fitted with the same style floor coverings). Cut strips of carpet to fill the void, taking care to install the patch with the nap facing the same direction. Use a carpet seamer (inset photo) to bond the carpet patch.

Carpet seamer

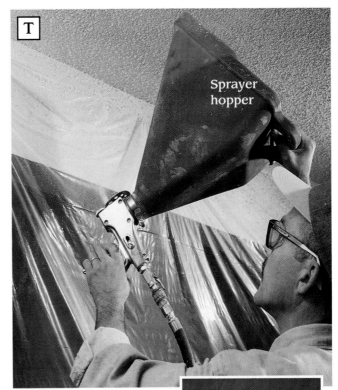

FIGURE S: Mix dry ceiling texture with clean water, according to the instructions on the bag, blending to achieve the proper consistency for spraying.

21 Creating a smooth seam between the beam and the ceiling can be tricky, especially if the ceiling has a textured covering (as in the project shown here). In this case, we started by scraping the texturing material off the ceiling near the beam so the joint compound would be able to bond effectively at the seam. Scrape back at least 1 ft. **(See FIGURE Q).** Next, we laid a bed of joint compound on both sides of the seam and pressed creased paper wallboard tape into the seam **(See FIGURE R).** We smoothed out the tape with a 6-in. wallboard knife. Apply joint compound and tape as needed to cover all wallboard seams and screw heads. It generally takes three applications of joint compound with successively broader wallboard knives to create taped seams that are ready for sanding and finishing.

22 When patching a textured ceiling, you'll get the best results using a rented texture sprayer (See inset photo, right). Texture sprayers are self-contained units with a compressor and spray gun designed specifically for applying ceiling texture. Ask for usage instructions at your rental center. You can try painting texture on, but it's very difficult to get it to blend with the original texture. Mix dry ceiling texture with clean water, according to the instructions on the bag, to achieve the proper consistency for spraying **(See FIG-URE S).** A power mixing accessory chucked in your power drill speeds up the mixing process.

FIGURE T: Texture sprayers (inset photo) are the best tools for achieving professional ceiling texture results. They can be rented at most rental stores, and the dry ceiling texture can be purchased at most building centers. Be sure to protect the surrounding areas adequately before spraying ceiling texture. Make sure the surrounding ceiling area is clean, and spray light coats where the newly textured ceiling meets the old to try and get them to blend together.

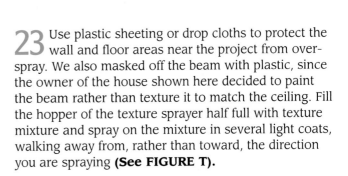

23 Use plastic sheeting or drop cloths to protect the wall and floor areas near the project from overspray. We also masked off the beam with plastic, since the owner of the house shown here decided to paint the beam rather than texture it to match the ceiling. Fill the hopper of the texture sprayer half full with texture mixture and spray on the mixture in several light coats, walking away from, rather than toward, the direction you are spraying **(See FIGURE T).**

24 Finish patching-in in the project area by painting wallboard and patching floor coverings (See *TIP*, previous page).

Windows

The number, style and condition of your home's windows go a long way toward setting the overall feeling it conveys. Expansive, well-kept windows placed strategically throughout the house bring in natural light and make for a brighter home that seems inviting and spacious. Conversely, small, poorly located windows or windows that have fallen into disrepair send an unfriendly, dreary message to visitors and occupants alike. A worn-out window with cracked glass, peeling paint and shoddy hardware will affect your perspective as you look out through it. And if it doesn't operate smoothly, it will challenge you every time you try to bring a breath of fresh air into your home.

Replacing a worn-out window is a simple remodeling project that yields big results: New windows are easier to maintain and clean, energy efficient and will add to the beauty and value of your home. Replacing a window with a larger model will yield the same results, but on an even greater scale. For more ambitious handymen, installing a bay window or skylight can transform an ordinary or dark room into a luxurious, inviting living space. In the following section, you'll find all the information you need to change your outlook by upgrading your windows.

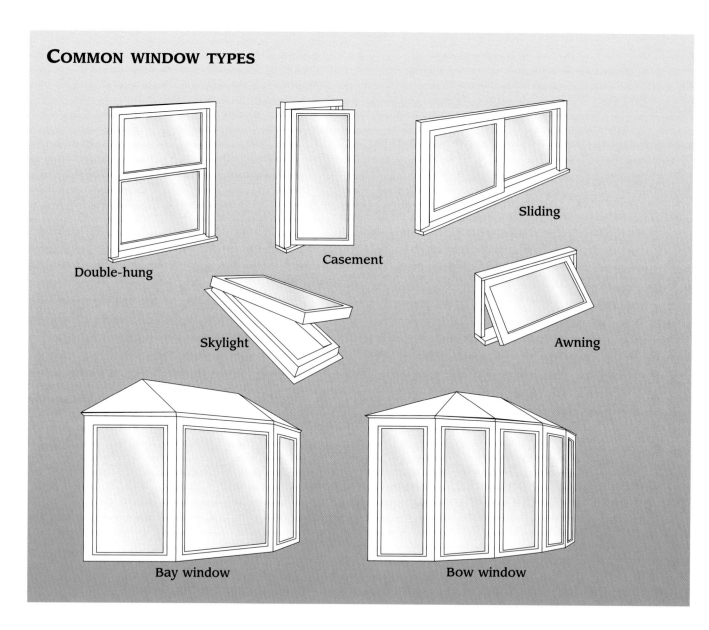

Double-hung

Casement

Sliding

Skylight

Awning

Bay window

Bow window

Window Basics

On an elemental level, a window is simply a framed piece of glass that's mounted in an opening in an exterior wall. In most windows, the glass frame can be moved up or down or swung out to create ventilation in a room. When closed, the glass allows light to pass in and out of a room, while keeping the effects of the weather safely outdoors.

But on a more sophisticated level, windows are key features in your house design, and they greatly affect how your house looks and functions. While the primary purpose of a window is practical, most window remodeling projects are undertaken as much for aesthetic goals as for practical considerations. For this reason, the range of styles, sizes and designs has increased greatly in recent years. And along with

changing designs, manufacturers have made important advances in window technology to make installation easier for the home handyman. Much like prehung doors that are purchased already mounted on the door jamb frame, most windows today are sold with preattached brick mold or nailing flanges that attach to the rough opening frame to secure the window unit.

Window types. The simplest windows are *fixed windows*—they don't open and close and therefore contain no moving parts. A familiar example of a fixed window is the picture window. Common *operating window* types include double-hung windows, casement windows, awning windows, sliding windows and roof

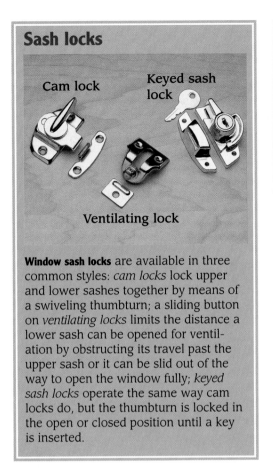
windows (skylights). When joined together into banks, many of these window types can be used to create *bay windows* or *bow windows*. Double-hung, casement and fixed windows are the most common window types used for bay windows.

Parts of a window.

• *Sash:* A framed, movable glass pane.

• *Light:* An individual piece of glass bordered by a frame.

• *Rail:* One of the horizontal members forming a sash frame.

• *Stile:* One of the vertical members forming a sash frame.

• *Muntins:* The narrow cross-hatch strips that divide a multi-light sash. Muntins may be individual separation strips or a preassembled wood or plastic grille that is overlaid on the glass to create the appearance of a multi-light sash.

• *Jambs:* The horizontal and vertical members creating the window frame, including the top or header jamb, the side jambs and the bottom jamb.

• *Case molding (Casing):* The mitered window trim that covers the front edges of the jambs. The interior casing includes

CROSS-SECTION OF A WINDOW (DOUBLE-HUNG)

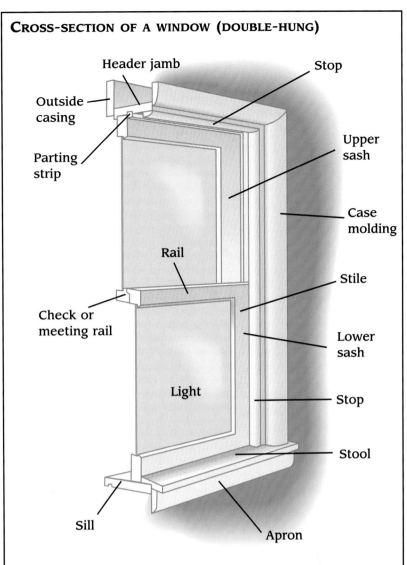

Header jamb
Stop
Outside casing
Parting strip
Upper sash
Case molding
Rail
Stile
Check or meeting rail
Lower sash
Light
Stop
Stool
Sill
Apron

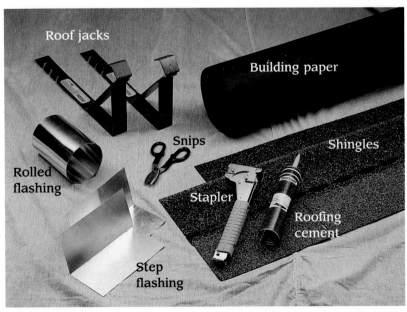

Roof jacks

Building paper

Snips

Shingles

Rolled flashing

Stapler

Roofing cement

Step flashing

Roofing and flashing is an important part of some window projects, namely bay window and skylight installation. Roof jacks provide a safe, temporary foothold for roof work.

Cripple studs

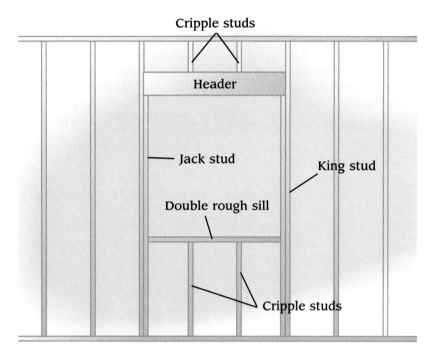

Header

Jack stud

King stud

Double rough sill

Cripple studs

Rough framing for a window is basically the same for all types—double-hung, casement, awning and the rest. A jack stud is installed next to the first full-length stud on each side of the wall opening. A header, usually made of doubled 2 × 4s or 2 × 6s, is attached to the wall studs at the top of the opening. A rough sill is installed directly beneath the header at the bottom of the rough opening. The cut-off studs above the header and beneath the sill are called cripple studs.

Safety tip

Apply wide masking tape diagonally across window sashes before removing or installing a window. In the event the glass should break, the tape will help contain the broken glass, minimizing the risk of cuts.

the header casing, the side casing and the bottom casing (sill and stool).

• *Stop molding:* Molding strips attached to the faces of the jambs to create surfaces for sashes to ride against.

• *Drip edge:* The metal cap fastened to the top edge of the window's outside casing to divert water past the window.

• *Flashing:* Metal or vinyl strips that seal the window and window rough opening from the elements.

• *Parting strip:* The narrow member that separates the upper and lower sash on a double-hung window.

Window options. In addition to basic considerations of style and size, there are a number of options you should consider before ordering new windows. If you are installing a new window into an existing opening, remove the case molding from inside to allow for more accurate measuring (See page 60).

Cladding is the general term used to identify the trim material used on the window. Most windows today are clad with either vinyl or aluminum for ease of maintenance and low cost. The cladding colors are limited to three or four stock colors, but you can special-order just about any color you like. Wood-clad windows are popular with owners of older homes. They're usually shipped with the wood primed and ready for painting.

Glazing is the term window and door manufacturers use for the glass they install in their product. Glazing options vary among manufacturers, but most offer single-, double- and triple-glazed windows (more glass layers mean higher energy efficiency). You can also order windows with glass that has been tinted, treated to filter out UV rays or reinforced with plastic film. The most efficient windows contain an inert gas (like argon) between glass panes.

Installation methods: New windows are outfitted with either a nailing flange or preattached brick mold. For most retrofit remodeling projects, windows equipped with nailing flanges are a good alternative because you can reuse your existing brick mold (instead of cutting out siding for new brick mold that will likely be a different size and style from the original brick mold).

Window Replacement

Perhaps more than any other part of your house, windows take a beating. Condensation, direct exposure to the elements, and ongoing use combine to shorten the life span of even the best-quality windows. As a result, replacing windows is one of the most common home remodeling projects.

Whenever possible, replace a window with one that's the same size. Even if that means custom-ordering a window unit versus buying one off the floor, the time and work you'll save is usually worth the extra expense because you won't need to cut open the wall or install new framing.

The project shown in this chapter involves retrofitting a larger window, which is an option you may want to consider for aesthetic or ventilation reasons. Although some demolition and new framing is involved, the benefits of having a larger window outweighed the extra costs and effort.

Rough openings, (shaded here in red), should be ½ to 1 in. larger than the outside dimensions of the window unit in each direction. This will create gaps of ¼ to ½ in. on all sides, which should be enough room to adjust the window so it's square in the rough opening. Window manufacturers specify the required rough opening for framing a window in the installation instructions.

FIGURE A: Pry off the case molding around the window with a flat pry-bar. Work carefully to avoid damaging the surrounding wall surfaces.

FIGURE B: Locate the nearest wall stud outside the rough opening area, and draw a cutting line on the wallboard that's centered over the wall stud. This will provide nailing surfaces for the new wallboard.

Replacing a window

The following project shows how we replaced an old double-hung with a larger, more energy-efficient unit. If you're making a one-for-one replacement with a window of the same size, skip the demolition and framing information (unless the condition of the framing members requires that you replace them).

1 Pry off the case molding around the window with a flat prybar **(See FIGURE A).** Use care when handling the case molding so you can reuse it around the new window. Also use care to avoid damaging the surrounding wall surfaces. If you plan to remove more than one wall stud, construct a temporary support wall to support the ceiling joists until the new window header is installed (See page 13).

2 If you need to enlarge the window opening, mark the rough opening for the new window on the wall. The rough opening should be ½ to 1 in. larger than the window in height and in width.

3 Locate the closest framing members outside the layout lines, using an electronic stud finder **(See**

Tools you'll use:
- Utility knife
- Flat prybar
- Reciprocating saw
- Circular saw
- Hand saw
- Level
- Drill/driver
- Hammer and nail set
- Staple gun

Materials list:
- Window and brick mold
- Wood shims
- Wallboard, screws and finishing supplies
- Dimension lumber and case molding
- Nails (10d casing, 10d and 8d common and 6d casing)
- Fiberglass insulation
- Drip edge molding
- Caulk and panel adhesive

FIGURE B). Score cutting lines directly over the center of the framing member, using a utility knife (this will allow you to use the existing framing member as nailing strip when patching in new wallboard). With a flat prybar, or by hand-pulling, remove the wallboard or

FIGURE C: Remove the old window unit. To simplify the process, remove the sashes from the frame first. Free the frame by cutting nails that attach the frame to the wall studs with a reciprocating saw.

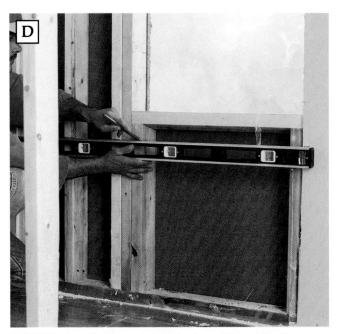

FIGURE D: Use a level as a straightedge for marking cutting lines on the wall studs in the project area. Allow space for the new sill and header when laying out the cuts.

plaster around the window up to the scored lines. If necessary, clean up the edges of the cut over the framing members with a utility knife and straightedge.

4 Apply thick masking tape over the window glass (See *Safety tip,* page 58) and remove the sashes from the window frame. Cut through the nails that hold the frame in the rough opening with a reciprocating saw and remodeler's blade. Tip the old window frame out of the opening **(See FIGURE C).**

5 If enlarging the rough opening, use a level to mark the new rough opening height on the framing members in the project area **(See FIGURE D).** Your reference lines should allow for a new header (See page 58), a double rough sill, and the jack and king studs.

6 Cut the wall studs on the rough opening lines, using a reciprocating saw **(See FIGURE E).** Pry the cut framing members loose from the exterior wall sheathing with a hammer and flat prybar and remove them.

FIGURE E: After installing temporary support, cut the wall studs to create the rough opening. Remove enough of each stud to allow for the sill and header. Avoid damage to the sheathing as you remove the studs.

FIGURE F: Nail a jack stud to each king stud on either side of the rough opening, using 10d nails spaced every 12 in. Jack studs extend from the wall's sole plate to the bottom of the planned header location.

FIGURE G: Construct a header: We sandwiched a strip of ⅜-in. plywood between two pieces of 2-in. dimension lumber, then bonded the header with construction adhesive and 10d nails.

7 Mark the positions of new framing members (king studs and jack studs), if needed, on the sole plate. Install the king stud by toe-nailing it into the sole plate with 10d common nails. Use a level to plumb the king stud, then toe-nail it to the cap plate.

8 Cut 2 × 4 jack studs to fit from the sole plate to the bottom of the planned header location. Attach the jack studs by face-nailing them to the king studs every 12 in. on both sides of the rough opening with 10d common nails **(See FIGURE F).** Keep the edges of the jack studs flush with the edges of the king studs.

9 Construct a header from dimension lumber and plywood or engineered beam stock (See *Chart, right,* and also check with your local building inspector). For the installation shown here, we sandwiched a piece of ⅜-in. plywood between two pieces of 2-in. dimension lumber **(See FIGURE G).** Bond the beam with construction adhesive and 10d common nails. Drive nails in a staggered pattern into both faces of the header.

10 Set the header into place on top of the jack studs. Make sure it's resting cleanly on the studs and the front face is flush with the front edge of the studs. Double-check the header with a level, and correct by driving wood shims between the low end and

Window header construction

Rough opening width	Material
Up to 3 ft.	Two 2 × 4s, ⅜-in. plywood spacer
3 ft. to 5 ft.	Two 2 × 6s, ⅜-in. plywood spacer
5 ft. to 7 ft.	Two 2 × 8s, ⅜-in. plywood spacer
7 ft. to 8 ft.	Two 2 × 10s, ⅜-in. plywood spacer

the top of the jack stud. Attach the header by nailing through the king studs and into the ends of the header with 10d common nails **(See FIGURE H).** Toe-nail through the cripple studs into the top of the header.

11 Cut a 2 × 4 to fit between the jack studs. Face-nail it to the tops of the cripple studs beneath the window opening, checking to make sure it's level. Cut a second 2 × 4 the same length and face-nail it to the lower 2 × 4 **(See FIGURE I)** to form a double rough sill. Even though some building codes may not require

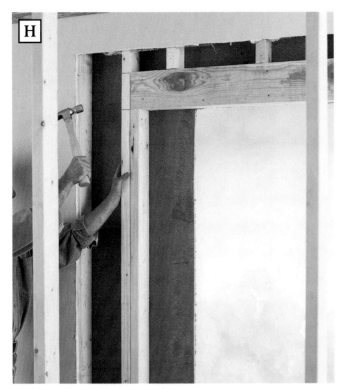

FIGURE H: Set the header in position at the top of the window opening, and attach it by driving 10d nails through the king studs and into the ends of the header.

FIGURE I: Attach the double rough sill in two pieces. Cut two 2 × 4s to fit the width of the rough opening, then nail one of the 2 × 4s to the tops of the cripple studs. Face-nail the second 2 × 4 to the first one.

a double sill for smaller windows, it's always a good idea to use them.

12 Enlarge the opening in the exterior sheathing and siding to match the window rough opening. Begin by drilling or driving nails through the sheathing and siding at the corners of the rough opening **(See FIGURE J).** Connect the holes with a pencil and straightedge to form an outline of the rough opening.

NOTE: *If your house has wood, vinyl or metal siding, cutting through the siding to enlarge a window opening isn't especially difficult. But if your siding is masonry-based (stucco or brick veneer), you're looking at a fairly challenging project if you decide to enlarge the opening. See page 134 for more information on cutting openings in various siding materials.*

13 Mount a remodeler's blade in your circular saw and set the cutting depth so the saw will cut slightly deeper than the combined thickness of the siding and the sheathing. Retract the blade guard on the saw, let it build to full speed, set the tip of the saw foot firmly on the siding and ease the blade down into and through the siding, making a plunge cut. Cut as far as you can on the straight runs **(See FIGURE K)** without cutting beyond the outline corners. Finish the cuts at the corners with a reciprocating saw or a hand saw.

FIGURE J: Drill holes through the exterior sheathing and siding at the four corners of the rough opening (See also FIGURE K) and connect the four holes with a straightedge. Cut the siding and sheathing along the reference lines with a circular or reciprocating saw.

FIGURE K: Remove siding and sheathing in the new rough opening area by cutting with a circular saw, then finishing the cuts with a chisel.

FIGURE L: Set the new window into the opening, then shim it from inside until it's level and plumb in the opening.

FIGURE M: Trace the outline of the brick mold onto the siding to scribe a cutting line, then remove the window from the opening.

14 Remove the new window from the packaging and test-fit it into the window opening **(See FIGURE L).** From inside, drive wood shims between the window jambs and the rough opening members until the window is level and plumb in the opening.

15 For windows with preattached brick mold, trace the outline of the brick mold onto the siding around all four sides of the window, then remove the window from the opening. For windows with nailing flanges and no preattached brick mold, use a scrap piece of the brick mold you'll be installing as a spacer and trace around the perimeter of the window unit (See page 134). Set a circular saw to a depth that will just cut through the siding, down to the sheathing beneath it **(See FIGURE M).** Plunge-cut through the siding along the brick mold outline. Stop the cuts just short of the corners and square them up with a chisel.

16 Cut 8-in.-wide strips of building paper and insert one edge of the paper between the siding and the exposed sheathing on all four sides of the window opening. Wrap the paper around the framing studs and staple it inside the opening **(See FIGURE N).**

17 Cut a piece of metal drip edge to fit the width of the window opening and slide it into place between the siding and building paper at the top **(See**

FIGURE O). Do not secure it in place with fasteners.

18 **For windows with preattached brick mold:** Apply panel adhesive to the back edges of the brick mold and set the window into the opening so the drip edge overlaps it at the top. Reinstall shims to bring the unit back to level and plumb. Drive 10d galvanized casing nails through the brick mold and into the wall framing **(See FIGURE P). For windows with nailing flanges:** Set the window in the opening and shim. Drive 8d common nails through the guide holes in the flanges and into the framing members. Miter-cut the brick mold to fit, apply panel adhesive to the back edge of each piece, and attach the brick mold with 10d casing nails.

19 Nail the jambs to the wall framing at each shim location with 8d casing nails. Trim the shims flush with the surrounding wall surfaces, using a hand saw. Fill the gaps between the window and the rough opening framing members with fiberglass insulation.

20 Fill in wallboard around the project area, then tape, sand and paint the wall surface. Miter-cut case molding with 45° corners to frame the window jamb **(See FIGURE Q).** Attach the case molding with 6d finish nails driven into the edges of the jambs.

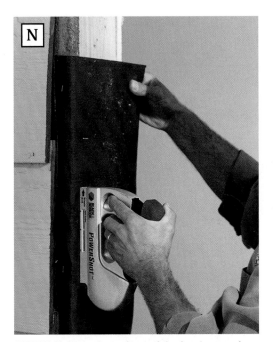

FIGURE N: Wrap the surfaces of the framing members in the rough opening with building paper. Tuck the edges of the strips behind the sheathing, and staple.

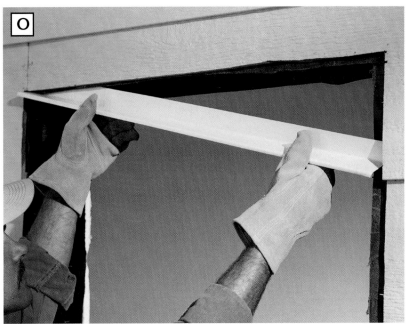

FIGURE O: Install drip edge above the window opening before permanently installing the window. Cut the drip edge to length and tuck it up between the siding and the sheathing. Don't use fasteners to attach drip edge: the siding pressure should hold it in place.

FIGURE P: Attach windows with preattached brick mold by driving 10d galvanized casing nails through the brick mold and sheathing and into the wall framing members. Drive the nail heads just below the surface with a nail set.

21 Seal the gaps around the brick mold and cover nails heads with paintable caulk.

FIGURE Q: Cut case molding to fit around the window (or reuse the original case molding, if it fits). The inside edges of the case molding (called the reveal) should be recessed slightly from the inside faces of the jambs. Drive nails into the jamb edges.

Interior view

Exterior view

Bay Windows

Bay windows add a new dimension to any room in your home. They project out from your walls and bring a piece of the great outdoors inside. Simply by replacing a plain picture window with an elegant bay window, you can transform a flat view into a three-dimensional panorama that puts your indoor living in a whole new light.

A bay window is almost a room of its own. The wide seat board can be fitted with a cushion to create a quiet window seat for reading or simply enjoying the sunshine. Or it can take on the look and feel of a greenhouse or solarium when it's appointed with a few well-chosen houseplants. Even viewed from outside your home, a bay window adds a touch of elegance that brings distinction to an otherwise ordinary house. If you've ever installed a new window or door, you already have most of the skills you need to install a new bay window yourself.

Bay window basics

Description. A bay window is a three-sided window structure with side sashes that project out from the exterior wall at an angle, then join with a larger picture window that's typically 15 to 24 in. away from the house. The individual sashes can be of just about any window type: casement, double-hung or fixed. The top of the bay window is treated in one of two ways: either a three-faced roof frame matching the profile of the window unit is added, or the window is connected directly to an overhanging soffit with vertical walls or trim boards. The area under the window unit can be treated with a short apron that covers a sturdy platform projecting out from the wall, or the apron may extend all the way or nearly all the way to the foundation of the house.

Window units that project out from the house in a smooth arc formed by multiple sashes are known as *bow windows* (See illustration, page 69). Bow windows generally are longer than bays, but the installation techniques are nearly identical.

Specifications. True bay windows are generally at least 60 in. wide and a minimum of 42 in. high—most are in a horizontal configuration. The side sashes on shorter bay windows generally angle inward at 45° to maximize the size of the main window at the front of the unit, while still allowing for full projection away from the house. On longer bay windows, the side sashes project out at a shallower 30° angle and are usually closer in size to the main window, resulting in a window unit that has a more symmetrical appearance.

Support systems. Bay windows usually rely on the structural bearing of the wall they're installed into for support. Until recent years, the most common support method was to attach a sturdy platform with angled braces to the wall framing members or rim joist. Variations to this method included the use of heavy iron support braces bolted to the wall or rim joist, or extending the floor joists outward to support the unit from below (See next page). Today, however, professional window installers most often use a cable system to provide support to the unit from above. The cables are attached to the wall members above the window, then

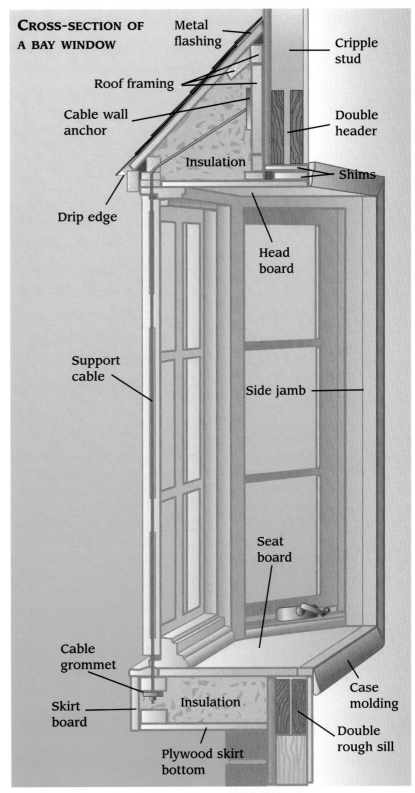

CROSS-SECTION OF A BAY WINDOW

Metal flashing

Cripple stud

Roof framing

Cable wall anchor

Double header

Insulation

Shims

Drip edge

Head board

Support cable

Side jamb

Seat board

Cable grommet

Case molding

Skirt board

Insulation

Double rough sill

Plywood skirt bottom

Bay windows are relatively complex units (and that's usually reflected in the price tag). The window unit shown above is similar to the bay window you'll see installed later in this chapter. The framing members around the perimeter of the rough opening include a double header with a plywood spacer and a double rough sill. The roof frame is mounted to the top of the unit then shingled and flashed using standard roofing methods. This window unit is supported by a cable system anchored to the wall of the house and threaded all the way through the front of the unit.

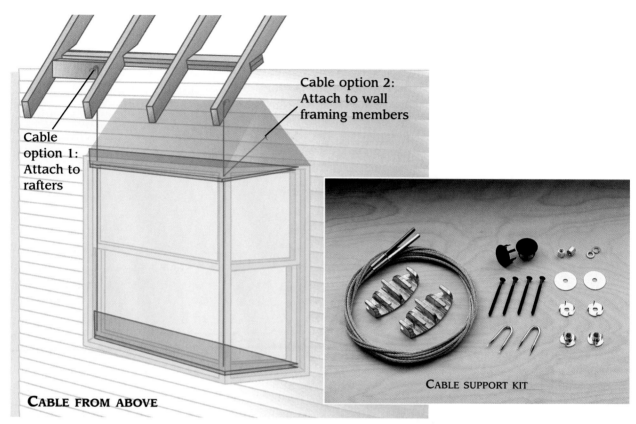

Cable option 1: Attach to rafters

Cable option 2: Attach to wall framing members

CABLE FROM ABOVE

CABLE SUPPORT KIT

Cable kits for installing and supporting bay window units eliminate the need for structural framing underneath. Braided steel cables (See inset photo) are threaded through concealed channels in the window framing and tie off to metal wall anchors that are attached to the wall studs. If the window is installed beneath a soffit or rafter overhang, you can attach the cables to the rafter ends, then install skirting between the top of the window and the soffit or rafter area. Cable-supported windows can be adjusted up or down slightly during installation by tightening or loosening hex nuts threaded to the ends of the cables underneath the window.

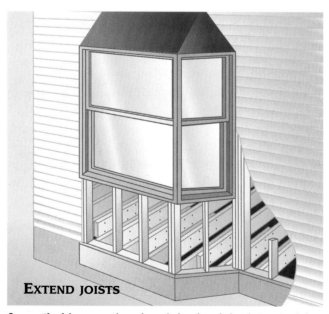

EXTEND JOISTS

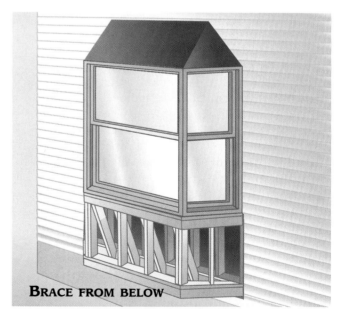

BRACE FROM BELOW

One method for supporting a bay window from below is to extend the floor joists out from the house and under the new window to serve as the base for a support platform. The joist extensions overlap the joists and are bolted to them—called "sistering"—and a skirt is framed up to the window from the extended joists (similar to a short wall).

Another option for supporting bay windows from beneath is to attach angled braces, made from dimension lumber, that extend from the bay to the rim joist of the house. A framed skirt hides the braces and serves as a nailing structure for sheathing and siding.

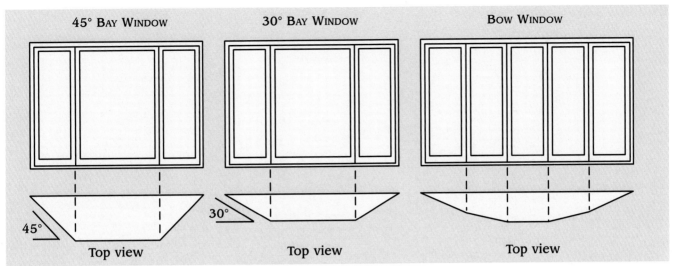

45° BAY WINDOW   **30° BAY WINDOW**   **BOW WINDOW**

45°

30°

Top view   Top view   Top view

Bay windows come in a variety of window sash configurations and styles to suit different installation requirements and house styles. Two common varieties are 45° bays (left) and 30° bays (center), that feature a large picture window in the center flanked by two narrower sash- es that may or may not open for ventilation. These bay styles get their names based on the angle the side panes face away from the house. Bow windows (right) offer a slim overall profile that's popular in more contemporary homes.

threaded through the front of the window inside the joints where the side sashes meet the front sash. The cable is then attached securely at the bottom of the window unit. Finding cable support systems for bay windows can take a little legwork, but most building centers that provide service to the building trades should be able to help out.

Accessories. In addition to cable support systems, you can also purchase custom-made roof frames built to match the dimensions of your window unit. These frames save time (and frustration) and assure satisfactory results.

Ordering a bay window. Bay windows are almost always special-order items that take two to four weeks for delivery. When ordering your bay window, you'll be asked to make some basic style choices, including: casement vs. double-hung, 30° vs. 45°, exterior trim color, whether to add grilles, and what type of glass to use. If you're replacing a picture window with a bay, take jamb-to-jamb and sill-to-header measurements of the existing window. Bay windows are manufactured in many sizes, but you may not be able to get one that fits the rough opening exactly. In

such a case, order the closest smaller size and plan on adding framing to the rough opening to bring it to the correct size for the new window unit. Also make sure the clerk helping you with your order knows what kind of siding you have. If the window opening is framed with masonry veneer, the window should be sized somewhat smaller so the preattached brick molding can fit inside the masonry veneer—if you use the rough opening dimensions as a guide, you'll have to remove the molding before installation (a bad idea) or trim the bricks all around the window opening.

BAY WINDOW ROOF FRAME

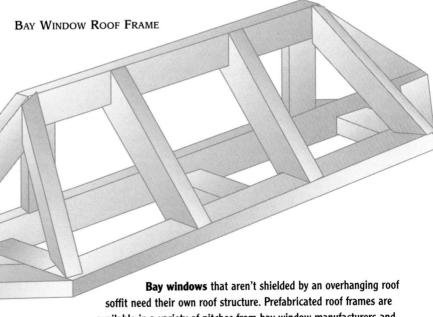

Bay windows that aren't shielded by an overhanging roof soffit need their own roof structure. Prefabricated roof frames are available in a variety of pitches from bay window manufacturers and can be ordered as an option with the window. Or you can construct your own from dimension lumber (See page 74).

FIGURE A: To take accurate measurements of your old window, first remove the case molding, then measure from the outside edges of jambs, sills and header to find the exact size of the old unit. You may even be able to access the existing rough opening, which is the best measurement to use when ordering a replacement window.

FIGURE B: Lay out positions for new framing members on the sill plate and on the header. Note the bevel drawn on the outer edge of the jack stud outline shown above.

Installing a bay window

Even if you're replacing an existing window of the same size, installing a bay window is a relatively involved remodeling project. In addition to the basic carpentry skills you'd use for any window or door installation, it requires basic roofing and roof framing skills and some trim carpentry. And because the assembled bay window units are quite heavy, you'll need to arrange for a helper or two, especially when setting and securing the unit in the rough opening. If you're enlarging an existing window opening, you'll need to cut wall framing members, which requires a building permit in most areas (even if you're doing a one-for-one replacement, it's always a good idea to run your plan past your local building inspector). But despite all the work, planning and expenses that go into a bay window project, you'll be making a major improvement that provides satisfaction and can create an instant increase in the value of your house.

1 Take careful measurements of the existing window before ordering your bay window unit. Remove the case molding and measure from the outsides of the

Tools you'll use:

In addition to the tools already listed for window installation (see page 60), you'll also need a jack, a table saw and a ladder.

Materials list:

Additional materials needed for bay window installation include:
- Rolled metal flashing
- Metal step flashing
- 4- or 6-mil plastic sheeting
- exterior-rated plywood (½- or ¾-in. thick)
- shingles
- roofing nails
- drip edge
- building paper
- roofing cement

jambs and the header and sill **(See FIGURE A)**. Also measure the thickness of the wall and make a note of the type of exterior siding you have (See *Ordering a bay window,* page 69). If you're enlarging an existing window opening, use an electronic stud finder to locate the framing members in the planned project area. Base the length of your window on the wall stud spacing, allowing for a new jack stud on each side of the rough opening and an inch for the required gap between the window unit and the jack studs. This will minimize the number of studs you'll need to cut.

2 When your window unit arrives, measure it immediately to make sure it's the size you ordered. If the size is incorrect, you're much better off finding out before you remove the old window.

3 Remove the old window by cutting through the nails that attach the jambs to the surrounding framing, using a reciprocating saw (See *Replacing a Window,* pages 60 to 65). For safety, remove the sashes from the old window frame first.

4 Add strips of dimension lumber, if necessary, to bring the rough opening to the correct size for your new window (or if your existing sill is too weak, check the installation directions for sill size requirements). If you need to decrease the height of the rough opening, shim up the height of the rough sill by adding a 1 × 6 or 2 × 6 on top of the rough sill. Mark layout lines on the new sill for adding vertical framing members to decrease the opening width. *NOTE:* Most bay windows require that the jack studs be beveled on the outer, inside edges. In our project, we needed to add vertical framing members anyway, so we noted the bevel cut on the layout lines **(See FIGURE B)**. If your rough opening is approximately the correct width, the easiest solution is to remove the existing jack studs and replace them with beveled jack studs.

5 Bevel-rip new jack studs at the angle suggested by the window manufacturer. We used a portable table saw to bevel-rip the 2 × 6 jack studs needed for our installation **(See FIGURE C)**.

6 Attach additional framing members and the new jack studs securely to the surrounding framing with 3-in. galvanized deck screws **(See FIGURE D)**. Bore pilot holes first to make driving the screws easier.

7 Staple sheet plastic over the rough opening before beginning exterior work.

FIGURE C: Jamb angles vary from manufacturer to manufacturer (check the instructions), but frequently you'll need to cut a bevel on the outer edges of the jack studs. We used a portable table saw for the chore.

Beveled jack stud

FIGURE D: Attach additional rough framing members and the jack studs securely to the surrounding framing with 3-in. deck screws.

FIGURE E: If you're planning to install a small roof to cover the new bay window, remove any siding or trim in the roof installation area. Take care not to damage the materials. Matching siding and trim with new materials can be next to impossible.

FIGURE F: Wrap exposed framing members with building paper secured with staples. Slip the edges of the building paper strips between the siding and the wall sheathing.

Masonry clip

FIGURE G: Attach masonry clips to the side jambs of the bay window unit if it will be installed into an opening with a masonry exterior. Masonry clips allow the window to be secured to the rough opening members from inside the house.

FIGURE H: Set the window into the opening and support it temporarily from beneath with 2 × 4 braces. A jack with a wood post and T-brace can be used to adjust the height of the window easily. Make sure the T-brace is centered.

8 Remove any siding or trim that will interfere with the installation of the window unit, the roof, or any skirting beneath the unit **(See FIGURE E).** Leave the wall sheathing intact. Follow the same procedure for doing this as outlined in the section on replacing a window, pages 60 to 65. If you're removing multiple pieces of siding or trim, number them in correct sequence on the back side as you remove them.

9 Line the rough opening with strips of building paper. Tuck the edges between the sheathing and siding, and staple the strips to the framing members in the rough opening **(See FIGURE F).**

10 If the the siding around the rough opening is brick veneer or another masonry product, attach metal masonry clips to the outsides of the jambs before setting the window unit in place **(See FIGURE G).** Bay windows are normally secured to the house by driving nails through the nailing flanges on the exterior side of the unit and into the wall framing members. With brick veneer, this can't be done unless you remove the bricks around the opening. Masonry clips provide a means to attach the window unit to the framing members inside the rough opening.

NOTE: *If you will be supporting the window unit from below, install your support system of braces or extended floor joists (See page 68) before setting the window into the opening. If using a cable system, as shown here, the support is not installed until after the window is in place.*

11 Make sure the rough opening is clear of debris, then set the window unit into the opening. You should have at least one helper (two is better) for this step. Also be prepared with a few 2 × 4s about 1 ft. longer than the distance of the window from the ground to use as braces. Slide the window in place until the nailing flanges or preattached brick mold contact the exterior wall surface. If the exterior is brick veneer, slide the unit into the opening until the trim at the top of the unit strikes the exposed sheathing above the window opening. Slip 2 × 4 braces under the front edge of the unit to prop it up. To make it easier to raise or lower the unit when plumbing it in the opening, place a jack and wood brace assembly below the front, center of the window **(See FIGURE H).**

12 Shim around the rough opening from the inside until the window is centered in the opening and is plumb and square.

13 If you have non-masonry siding, the nailing flanges or brick mold should be flat against the wall sheathing. If flanges or brick mold are overlapping the siding, trace around it, then remove the win-

FIGURE I: Secure the window in the opening. Masonry clips are shown here, but you'll likely nail it through flanges or brick mold.

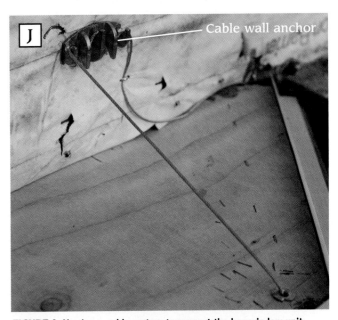

Cable wall anchor

FIGURE J: If using a cable system to support the bay window unit, attach the anchoring devices at wall framing member locations aligned as closely as possible to the front corners of the unit.

FIGURE K: Cable-supported bay windows can be raised or lowered by tightening or loosening the nuts securing the cable bottoms.

FIGURE L: Staple a 4- or 6-mil plastic vapor barrier to the top of the window. Build a roof frame from dimension lumber and screw it to the wall at stud locations. If you buy a preassembled roof, attach it using the same procedure.

FIGURE M: Bend light-gauge metal strip flashing to form drip edge, then insert the drip edge between the siding and sheathing above the roof. Friction-fitting it behind the siding should hold the drip edge in place without the need for fasteners.

FIGURE N: Fill the roof cavity with fiberglass insulation. Cut roof sheathing into pieces to create a roof deck. Make sure the joints between sheathing strips fall over nailing strips or framing members.

FIGURE O: Trim sections of standard drip edge to fit around the bottom edges of the roof deck. Nail the strips in place with roofing nails driven close to the top of each strip. Fold overlapping corners over the bottom strip.

dow and trim away the siding (see page 64). Reinstall and shim the window unit.

14 Secure the window in the opening by screwing masonry clips to the framing members **(See FIGURE I),** or by driving 10d casing nails through the nailing flanges or brick mold and into the wall framing members.

15 Attach permanent supports **(See FIGURE J).** If using a cable system, install the kit components and attach the cable to the anchoring brackets according to the directions that come with the kit. Be sure the anchors are connected to wall framing members, and arrange them so neither the hardware nor the cables will interfere with the window roof.

16 Adjust the window up or down by tightening or loosening the adjustment nuts that thread to the bottom of each cable, near the grommet **(See FIGURE K).** Drive wood shims beneath the unit to level it if using lower supports. When the window is properly positioned, remove the jack and temporary brackets.

For soffit skirt installations. If you're closing off the top of the window unit by connecting it to your soffit overhang, simply make a 2× frame with the same dimensions and shape as the window unit top, and attach it to the soffit. Insert vertical nailing strips at the corners, insulate above the window, then clad the frame with siding material. Skip to step 28.

17 Begin building the roof. Staple a 4- or 6-mil plastic vapor barrier to the top of the window. Build a roof frame from 2× dimension lumber (or buy a pre-assembled roof frame) and screw it to the wall framing at stud locations with 3-in. galvanized wood screws **(See FIGURE L** and the *Illustration* on page 69).

18 Slip metal drip edge underneath the siding directly above the roof frame **(See FIGURE M).** Do not use fasteners. Fill the cavity with fiberglass insulation.

19 Cut plywood sheathing pieces to fit the frame. Screw them to the roof framing members **(See FIGURE N).**

FIGURE P: Staple building paper over the roof deck, starting at the bottom if multiple pieces of building paper are needed.

FIGURE Q: Cut a piece of step flashing to fit into the joint where each back corner meets the wall. Nail the step flashing near the top edge to the wall sheathing.

20 Trim sections of drip edge to fit around the bottom edge of the roof sheathing and nail them in place with roofing nails **(See FIGURE O).**

21 Staple building paper over the roof sheathing **(See FIGURE P).** Try to cover the entire roof with one continuous piece of roofing paper. If multiple pieces are needed, overlap joints by at least 5 in., with higher pieces overlapping the lower ones.

22 Attach a piece of step flashing at each bottom corner of the roof, where it meets the wall **(See FIGURE Q).** These end pieces of step flashing should extend ¼ in. beyond the drip edge. Trim with a tin snips so the overlap matches the angle of the drip edge. Nail the step flashing to the wall sheathing near the top edge.

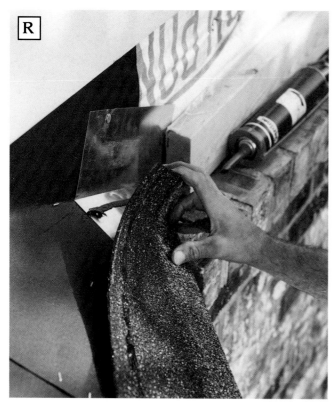

FIGURE R: Lay a starter course of 6-in.-wide shingle strips. Overlay the first piece of step flashing on each side.

FIGURE S: Nail a course of full-height shingles directly over the starter row, making sure the alignment notches do not align and the bottom edges are even with the bottom edges of the starter row.

FIGURE T: Continue shingling and flashing the roof, interweaving the shingle courses with the step flashing.

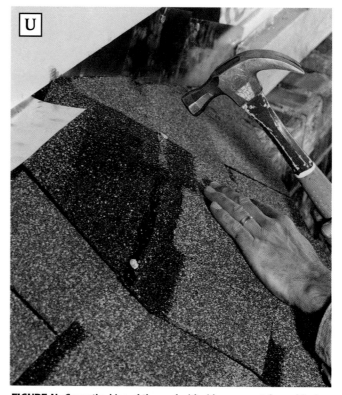

FIGURE U: Cover the hips of the roof with ridge caps cut from shingle tabs. Start at the bottom and work your way toward the top. Trim the top edge of the top shingle to fit.

23 Cut 6-in.-wide shingle strips for the starter row of shingles. Trim the edge that butts against the step flashing to fit into the corner. Apply a bead of roofing cement over the step flashing and lay the starter row of shingles in place **(See FIGURE R).** The shingles should extend ½-in. beyond the front edge of the drip edge. *Note: If you're not familiar with basic shingling and flashing techniques, check your local library or another Handyman Club book for more information on the subject.*

24 Nail a full row of shingles over the starter row so that the notches do not align and the bottom edges are even with the bottom edges of the starter row **(See FIGURE S).**

25 Set the second pieces of step flashing on each side of the roof. Overlap the pieces of step flashing by 5 in. Continue to apply roofing cement to each piece of step flashing and proceed up the roof to the top flashing with full rows of shingles, overlapping the notches of the previous row by ½ in. **(See FIGURE T).** Trim end shingles to fit against the wall.

26 Cover the hips of the roof with ridge caps made from 1-ft. lengths of shingle. Starting at the bottom, overlap and nail the ridge caps as with rows of full shingles **(See FIGURE U).**

27 Bend the drip-edge flashing inserted above the roof down over the top row of shingles. Nail the flashing to the top row of shingles with rubber-gasket nails **(See FIGURE V).** Bend the corners of the flashing over the hips as needed to match the contour of the roof.

28 Cover the top flashing with strips of shingle that extend ½ in. beyond the bottom edge of the drip-edge flashing **(See FIGURE W).** Secure the strips with a thick layer of roofing cement—don't use nails.

29 Since no support framing was required underneath this cable-hung bay, a short skirt and trim is all that is needed to conceal the cable adjust-

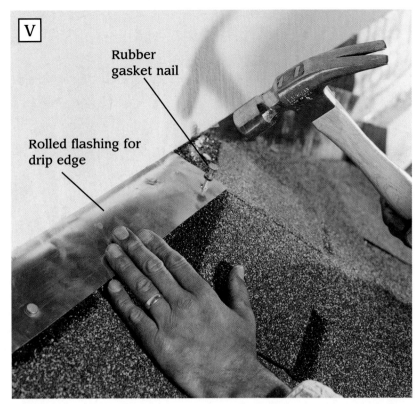

Rubber gasket nail

Rolled flashing for drip edge

FIGURE V: Nail the top flashing down to the top row of shingles with rubber-gasket nails. Bend the corners of the flashing to follow the contours of the roof.

FIGURE W: Conceal the drip-edge flashing by covering it with strips of shingles. Use a thick bead of roofing cement to attach the shingle strips.

FIGURE X: Make a frame to provide support for skirt boards and attach the frame to the bottom of the window unit.

FIGURE Y: After inserting insulation and a vapor barrier, cut a plywood cover to fit over the skirt frame opening. Attach the cover with deck screws.

FIGURE Z: The primary function of skirt boards is to conceal and seal the area containing the window support system. But choosing the right skirting can also add a dramatic accent to a bay window and further enhance your home's exterior details.

To complete the exterior of our bay window installation (left), brown-tinted siding caulk was used to conceal screw heads and to create a seal around the window unit.

(Below) **FIGURE AA:** Pack fiberglass insulation into the gaps between the window unit and the rough opening framing members.

ment rods. Attach a 2 × 4 frame to the bottom of the window 1 in. back from the front edges, using galvanized deck screws **(See FIGURE X).** Use a sliding T-bevel to transfer the correct cutting angles from the window unit to the frame boards.

30 Staple a 4- or 6-mil vapor barrier to the bottom of the seat board and fill the skirt cavity with fiberglass insulation. Cut strips of ½-in. plywood to cover the opening beneath the skirt area. Attach the plywood cover from below, using galvanized deck screws **(See FIGURE Y).**

31 Miter-cut skirt boards to fit over the skirt frame so that the corners fit tightly. The skirt boards should be wide enough to cover the skirt frame. In this installation, the skirt boards are cedar to match the cedar trim of the house. Fasten skirt boards to the frame with galvanized screws or nails **(See FIGURE Z).** Set the fastener heads below the surface and cover them with a paintable wood filler or caulk.

AA

FIGURE BB: If the window frame is not flush with the edges of the frame opening, measure the amount it's off, add the thickness of the wall covering, and rip-cut extension strips to shim out the parts of the window frame.

FIGURE CC: Drill countersunk screw pilot holes all the way through each extension strip, from edge to edge.

32 Caulk around the perimeter of the bay window, between the brick mold and the siding. For units with metal siding, use pre-tinted siding caulk that matches the cladding color. Caulk over all exposed screw heads and in any other area that might present a water entry point. This completes the exterior work for the installation.

33 From inside, trim all wood shims flush with the surrounding wall surfaces, using a hand saw. Pack fiberglass insulation into the cavities between the window unit and the rough opening members **(See FIGURE AA).** Do not pack the insulation too tightly or its insulating value will decrease.

34 In some bay window installations, the jambs, seat board and head board may not reach all the way to the interior-side edges of the rough opening framing members. This can happen if the wall is extra thick for soundproofing. It also results when a bay window is installed into a wall with a masonry veneer exterior. In such cases, there are several ways to address the problem. We chose to add extension strips

to the window frame pieces to bring them even with the edges of the framing members. To make extension strips, first measure the distance from the window frame parts to the front edges of the framing members **(See FIGURE BB).** Add the thickness of the wallboard that will be installed around the opening (usually ⅝ in. in newer homes). The total measurement equals the required width of the extension strips. Select clear stock of the same species as the frame material (usually oak or pine) and rip strips to the required width on your table saw. Cut them to match the length of each frame piece.

35 Drill countersunk pilot holes all the way from edge to edge in each extension strip. This can be tricky—use your drill press if it's handy. The holes should be spaced at intervals of about 1 ft. **(See FIGURE CC).**

36 Hold or clamp the extension strips in position against the edges of the frame pieces and extend the pilot holes into the the window frame. Apply wood glue to both mating edges, then attach the extension

FIGURE DD: Edge-glue and screw the extension strips to the window frame parts. Make sure to extend the pilot holes into the frame parts before driving the wood screws.

FIGURE EE: Finish and trim the interior side, including patching the wall with wallboard, painting and finishing the surfaces and installing trim moldings.

strips to the frame edges with wood screws **(See FIGURE DD).** The heads of the screws should be set well into the edges of the extension strips.

37 After the glue dries, scrape off glue squeeze-out with a putty knife. Sand the joints, if necessary, so the extension strips are level with the frame pieces.

38 Staple plastic sheathing over the exposed insulation around the window frame. Cut strips of wallboard to fit between the edges of the existing wall covering and the outside faces of the window frame pieces. Attach the wallboard strips with wallboard screws **(See FIGURE EE).**

39 Patch the seams and nail holes in the wallboard (See pages 34 to 41), then paint the patched areas to match the surrounding walls.

40 Reinstall the case molding from the original window, if you wish. Otherwise, purchase new case molding to match the bay window trim and miter-cut it to fit around the bay window opening (See

page 65). Fasten it with finish nails, recess the nail heads with a nail set, and putty over the nail holes to conceal them.

41 Finish-sand all exposed wood surfaces, then wipe with a tack cloth. Apply your wood finish of choice. We used a light oak wood stain, followed by three coats of polyurethane varnish.

NOTE: Bay windows can be fitted with curtains or blinds if privacy is a concern for you. Simply take the measurements for the unit as if it were three separate windows and have blinds cut to fit those dimensions. Or, you may prefer to hang drapes or curtains over the entire unit.

Skylights flood a room with warm, natural light and convey the perception of more space, especially in kitchens, hallways and smaller bathrooms like the one shown here. When properly installed, skylights are as weathertight as top-quality windows and last just as long.

Before

Skylights

There was a time before the advent of electric lighting when skylights could be found in just about every home. But in the first part of the 20th century, the reliance on skylights as a light source began to fade, and midway through the century they'd come to be regarded as luxury items. Thanks to improved, more watertight skylight designs and the revived appeal of natural light, installing a skylight has become one of the most popular do-it-yourself home improvement projects.

Skylights, sometimes called *roof windows,* are designed to fit between rafters and trusses, so there is no need to cut any structural members when installing them. Even when installed in groups, skylights can be arranged to use the existing roof structure for support. The only times you need to cut rafters or trusses are when installing extra-wide skylights, or when the desired location for the skylight falls directly beneath a roof member.

Skylight types. Today, skylights for home installations are almost always purchased in kits that include the window unit, a flashing kit and any attachment hardware required. In some cases, a flashing kit can be purchased separately if it's not provided with the window. The more economical skylights are called *fixed skylights*—they can't be opened for ventilation, like *operating skylights.* Some remodelers prefer fixed skylights over operating skylights because they believe the fixed models are less likely to leak.

There may have been some truth to this bias at one time, but a correctly installed operating skylight should pose no greater risk of water entry. Avoid inexpensive opaque plastic skylights for home remodeling purposes. These lightweight products are best suited for warehouses, sheds and other types of unfinished space where energy efficiency isn't an issue.

Framing options. Skylights can be purchased off the floor at most building centers in standard 22½-in. widths designed to fit the space between roof trusses or rafters installed 24 in. on-center. Framing for these units amounts to simply adding headers and sills between the rafters or trusses to create a rough opening of the correct size.

Rafters can be cut and framed with headers and sills for installation of wider skylights. You'll likely need to add vertical studs between the header and sill to create the correct rough opening size. When rafters are cut, sister a new rafter to the rafters on each side of the window opening. NOTE: *Because truss integrity must be maintained, you should never cut away any portion of a roof truss. Structural damage to the roof or house may result if the trusses are altered.*

Shafts. A skylight shaft creates a four-sided space leading from the skylight to a hole cut into the ceiling. If the skylight is installed in a conventional roof, a light shaft must be built. If the skylight is installed in a cathedral or attic ceiling, where the ceiling material is attached directly to the undersides of the rafters, no light shaft is required.

A light shaft can be straight with walls at right angles to the ceiling, or flared so

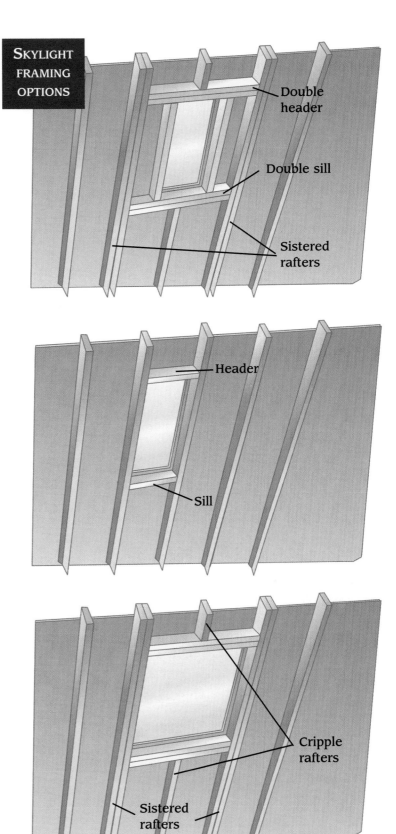

SKYLIGHT FRAMING OPTIONS

Double header

Double sill

Sistered rafters

Header

Sill

Cripple rafters

Sistered rafters

Skylight framing varies depending upon the width of the skylight and the construction of the roof. In cases where a portion of a rafter must be removed (top and bottom drawings), a new rafter is fastened to the old rafter (called "sistering") on either side of the window. A header and sill are installed between the cut ends of the rafter, creating cripple rafters above and below the window. Narrow skylights (center) often are sized to fit between two rafters.

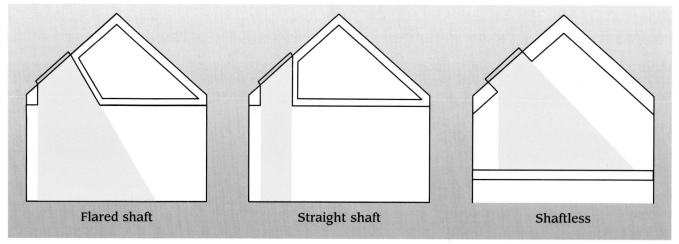

| Flared shaft | Straight shaft | Shaftless |

The shape of a skylight light shaft determines how much light the window can project into a room. A flared shaft (left) is longer at the base of the opening than the skylight. It takes greater advantage of the sun's path across the sky than a straight shaft (center). A straight shaft is preferable for a room with little ceiling space or if the construction of the roof area creates obstacles to a shaft, such as chimneys or vent stacks. Skylights installed in attic rooms or into cathedral ceilings (right) don't need light shafts, provided the ceiling is fastened directly to the rafters. In these instances, skylights take maximum advantage of sunlight because the light isn't restricted by the light shaft.

Operating skylights bring both fresh air and natural light into a room. Manufacturers offer crank extension kits so operating skylights can be opened from floor level. Some models are motor driven and can be opened and closed by remote control.

the opening in the ceiling is larger than the skylight opening. A flared shaft permits more sunlight entry and can direct the light to an area where it is needed. You can choose to flare anywhere from one to four of the shaft walls.

When designing a light shaft, compare the rafters or trusses to the ceiling joists. If they are parallel and aligned, you can install a shaft without having to cut any ceiling joists. If the joists are perpendicular to the rafters or trusses, you'll need to cut ceiling joists and install headers, sills and sisters, as when cutting rafters.

Roofing. Working on a roof to install a skylight is dangerous. Exercise caution and good judgment, and have a helper on hand at all times. In addition to the risk of bodily injury, there is also the risk of causing structural damage to your house by failing to create a watertight seal around the skylight, or by reinstalling the roofing materials improperly. In the project shown here, we provide basic instructions on how to remove and reinstall roof coverings, but if you don't have much experience, do additional research on the subject, or hire a roofing professional for that phase of the project.

Installing a skylight

A skylight installation project boils down to five main phases: planning, framing, installing the window unit, building the shaft, and trimming and fin-

A

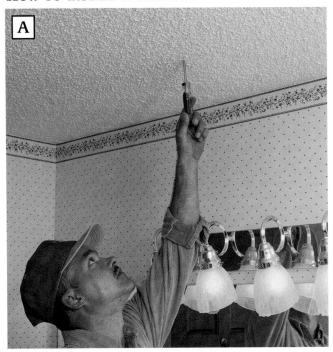

FIGURE A: Pierce a reference hole through the ceiling into the attic in the approximate center of the planned shaft opening location. The tip of the screwdriver will let you identify the joist cavity and rough location of the ceiling opening from above.

Tools you'll use:

In addition to the tools already listed for window installation in a wall (see page 60), you will need a ladder, a pair of metal roof jacks, a roofing knife or razor knife and a plumb bob.

Materials list:

Additional materials needed for a skylight installation include: 2-in. dimension lumber for sister rafters, joists, headers and sills, a 2 × 10 plank for the roof jacks, roofing cement and spreader, caulk gun, skylight flashings and roofing nails.

ishing. If your project will contain a light shaft (most will), carefully draw out a plan for the shaft framing. Because flaring the upper and lower side walls of the shaft greatly increases the amount of light the skylight introduces to the room, most installers choose to flare the shaft on at least the upper wall, but also on the lower wall if space allows. The net result of this is that the opening in the ceiling is longer than the opening in the roof sheathing where the skylight is secured.

B

Screwdriver puncture mark

FIGURE B: Find the midpoint between the ceiling joists in the center of the planned shaft opening area. Suspend a plumb bob from the roof sheathing until it hovers directly over the midpoint on the ceiling, and mark the roof sheathing at that point.

1 In the center of the approximate area where you plan to install the skylight, drive a screwdriver or nail up through the ceiling surface to establish a reference point **(See FIGURE A)**. Leave the screwdriver or nail in place, and locate the point from the attic area. You may need to remove floorboards and insulation to find the screwdriver shaft or nail point. The general area around it should be free from obstacles like vent stacks, wiring or ductwork.

2 Clear away any insulation to expose the entire project area. Draw a reference line between, and square to, the ceiling joists on each side of the project area. The line should run through the original puncture mark from the screwdriver or nail. Measure to find the midpoint of the reference line.

3 Use a plumb bob to find and mark a point on the roof sheathing, directly above the midpoint of the reference line **(See FIGURE B)**. Draw a line square to the rafters through the point.

FIGURE C: Measure out from the planned center of the rough opening in both directions, then mark the edges of the rough opening onto the roof sheathing.

Rough opening line

FIGURE D: Snap a chalk line between each corner of the rough opening and the corresponding corner of the shaft opening outline on the ceiling. The lines are used as a reference for installing the shaft frame.

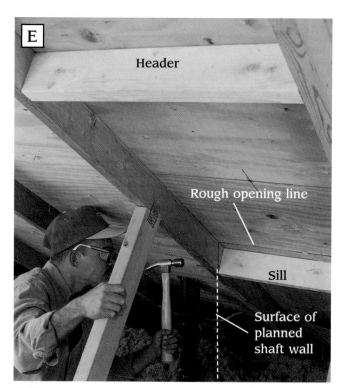

Header

Rough opening line

Sill

Surface of planned shaft wall

FIGURE E: Nail a sill and header between the roof trusses for the skylight. If the shaft will be flared, the leading edges of the sill and the header need to be set back from the surface of the planned shaft wall, or else you'll have to patch around them with wallboard.

FIGURE F: Make small adjustments to the rough opening width, if necessary, by attaching strips of plywood (called trimmers).

4 Outline the rough opening for the skylight on the underside of the roof sheathing. Measure out from the centerline equal amounts in each direction to mark the length of the opening **(See FIGURE C)**. The size of the rough opening should be listed in the installation information provided by the skylight manufacturer. Generally, a rough opening should be ½ to 1 in. larger in both directions than the actual size of the unit being installed.

5 Outline the ends of the ceiling opening on top of the ceiling material, according to your plan. If the opening will flare at both the top and bottom, try to locate the end lines so the pitch of the flare will be roughly equal at both ends of the shaft. But more importantly, make sure the ends of the ceiling opening are located in a position that makes sense for the room below. For example, in the project shown here a vent fan is located near the outside end of the ceiling area. We intentionally located the end of the ceiling opening so it wouldn't interfere with the vent fan.

6 Snap a chalkline from each corner of the rough opening to the corresponding corner on the ceiling opening outline **(See FIGURE D)**. The chalklines will be used as reference points for cutting and installing the shaft framing members. You may find it helpful to think of these chalklines as representing the inside wall surfaces of the light shaft.

7 Mark reference lines for a sill and a header at the top and bottom of the rough opening (you'll use 2× lumber the same width as the rafters to create the header and sill). Use a framing square to make sure the lines are perpendicular to the rafters. On flared shafts, the header and sill need to be positioned so they don't interfere with the wall covering you'll attach to the inside of the shaft frame. For most skylights, it's okay if the edges of the header and sill aren't flush against the ends of the rough opening area. Attach them with 10d nails driven through the rafters and into the ends of the header and sill **(See FIGURE E)**.

8 Install wood trimmers on the inside faces of the rafters, if necessary, to adjust the width of the rough opening **(See FIGURE F)**. This may be limited to adding a strip of plywood on each side, or you may have to nail "jack rafters" to the header and sill (called sistering) to frame the opening (See page 83).

9 Drill through the roof sheathing and shingles at the four corners of the rough opening **(See FIGURE G)** to establish a cutting outline for the rough opening.

10 Tack a 2 × 4 under the rough opening to catch the roof section when it's cut out **(See FIGURE H)**.

FIGURE G: Drill through the roof sheathing and shingles at each corner of the rough opening. The exit points of the drill bit will mark the rough opening corners on the exterior side of the roof.

FIGURE H: Attach a temporary brace underneath the rough opening area to catch the roof section after it is cut away from above.

11 Snap chalk lines on the roof to connect the four holes that mark the rough opening **(See FIGURE I).** Be sure to establish a safe foothold while working on the roof. Use roof jacks and a 2 × 10 to form a sturdy ledge (See page 57). On a steeply pitched roof, rent and wear appropriate fall-arresting gear and follow all safety precautions for its use.

12 Use a circular saw fitted with a remodeler's blade to cut along the chalked outline **(See FIGURE J).** Set the blade depth to cut completely through the shingles and roof sheathing in one pass. *Tip: Slip a strip of plywood next to the cutting line to serve as a cutting guide and to protect the foot of the saw from the shingle surfaces.*

FIGURE I: Outline the rough opening on the exterior of the roof, using a chalkline snapped between corners. For safe footing, use roof jacks supporting a 2 × 10 ledge (See page 57). Avoid using red chalk in your chalk line—it can stain shingles permanently.

FIGURE J: Cut out the rough opening with a circular saw. Use a remodelers blade, since you'll probably cut through metal fasteners. A strip of plywood makes a good straightedge and protects the saw foot from messy asphalt shingles.

FIGURE K: Wrap the framing members lining the rough opening with strips of building paper. Slip the building paper beneath the surrounding shingles.

FIGURE L: This skylight unit is set over the rough opening and fastened to the roof sheathing with mounting brackets that are attached to the skylight curb.

13 As a moisture barrier, slip 1-ft.-wide strips of building paper between the shingle layer and the roof sheathing, wrap them around the exposed framing members at the edges of the rough opening and staple them in place **(See FIGURE K).**

NOTE: Some skylight kits come with pre-attached cladding strips around the perimeter of the skylight curb. To install the skylight correctly, the wooden surfaces of the curb must be exposed. If your skylight has metal cladding around the top of the unit and the sides of the curb, remove the pieces before installing the unit and step flashing, then re-attach them (See step 18).

14 Set the skylight over the rough opening and check the fit. Most skylights sold in kit form today have L-brackets premounted to the curb. The free leaf of each L-bracket is connected directly to the roof sheathing. If your window comes with a preattached nailing flange instead of brackets, you may need to pry loose the shingles that surround the window with a flat prybar first. If the rough opening is sized correctly,

FIGURE M: Strips of building paper are wrapped around the skylight curb to keep moisture out. The strips are slipped beneath the adjoining shingles and building paper and run up near the top of the curb.

there will be a gap of about ½ in. between the edges of the rough opening and the skylight curb. When the skylight is set in proper position, attach it to the roof sheathing, positioning the fasteners over the building paper if possible **(See FIGURE L).**

15 Like any fixture you install on a roof, a skylight needs flashing to prevent water from penetrating around it. If your skylight came with a flashing kit, read the directions and make sure you understand the installation sequence before starting to install the flashing. In most cases, you begin by wrapping the skylight curb with strips of building paper about 10 in. wide. Each strip should be slipped underneath the adjoining shingles far enough so the other edge climbs up the curb almost to the top. Install the strips in this order: bottom, sides overlapping bottom, then top overlapping sides **(See FIGURE M).**

16 Flashing kits for skylights consist of a solid U-shaped piece of flashing for the sill and header, and step flashing for the sides of the unit. Begin instal-

FIGURE N: The sill flashing (part of the flashing kit provided with most skylights) is installed first. It fits around the bottom of the curb, and the ends of the flange are tucked under the first full course of shingles on each side. Nail the upright portions of the flanges to the curb with ¾-in. galvanized nails.

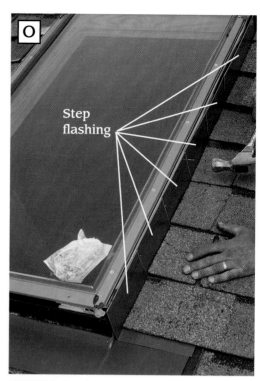

FIGURE O: Attach step flashing at the sides of the skylight, beginning at the bottom and working upward. Step flashing is woven into the shingle overlap pattern, and pieces overlap by about 5 in.

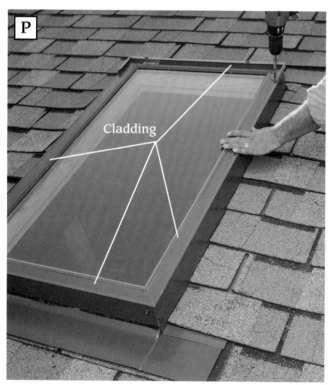

FIGURE P: Reattach the metal cladding pieces, starting from the bottom and working upward. The cladding should cover the tops of the sill flashing and the step flashing.

FIGURE Q: Install the head flashing over the cladding and step flashing, tucking the flange underneath the shingles and building paper above the skylight.

lation by applying a heavy layer of roof cement to the underside of the sill flashing, then slipping the flanges of the flashing up underneath the row of shingles along the bottom of the skylight. The base strip of the sill flashing should overlay the top row of shingles beneath the skylight (this directs water runoff over the shingles, not under them). Nail the vertical portions of the flanges to the skylight curb with ¾-in. galvanized nails driven as close to the top of the flashing as possible **(See FIGURE N).**

17 Secure the L-shaped pieces of step flashing along the sides of the skylight, using ¾-in. galvanized nails and roof cement. Begin installing the step flashing at the sill area. The bottom edge of the first piece of step flashing should be even with or slightly above the bottom of the skylight. The outer edge should be fitted beneath the first full shingle that butts up to the skylight unit. The second piece of step flashing should overlay both the first piece of flashing and the shingle above it, but it should underlay the next shingle. Each step flashing piece should overlap the lower piece by about 5 in. Install the step flashing in this manner all the way to the top on both sides of the skylight **(See FIGURE O).** Cut a slit at the corner of the top piece of step flashing, and bend it around the top of the curb.

18 Attach the cladding strips (See *NOTE,* page 89) that frame the bottom and sides of the skylight, covering the tops of the step flashing and sill flashing. Use the fasteners provided with the kit to attach the metal cladding strips (the unit shown here is attached with hex-head machine screws). Cover the tops of the step flashing and sill flashing. Attach the bottom piece of cladding first, then the sides, then the top **(See FIGURE P).**

19 Spread roofing cement on the bottom side of the head flashing and fit it around the top of the skylight. It should cover the cladding (in some cases it interlocks with the top cladding strip) and slip underneath the shingles and building paper at the top of the window. Screw the sides of the head flashing to the curb with ¾-in. galvanized screws **(See FIGURE Q).**

20 Begin to build the light shaft by installing a header and sill at the ends of the outline for the ceiling opening **(See FIGURE R).**

21 Drill through the ceiling at the four corners of the ceiling opening to mark its location in the room below **(See FIGURE S).**

22 Connect the four corner holes on the ceiling with chalk lines and remove the ceiling surface.

FIGURE R: Attach a header and sill between the ceiling joists to frame the shaft opening in the ceiling.

FIGURE S: Drill through the ceiling at each corner of the shaft opening to mark its location in the room below.

FIGURE T: Use a handsaw to make neat cutouts in wallboard ceilings. Start the cuts with a keyhole saw.

FIGURE U: Set corner posts in position against the rafters and joists, and mark cutting angles for trimming the posts.

Nailing strips

Corner post attached to truss web— NEVER CUT A TRUSS MEMBER

Front corner post removed for clarity

FIGURE V: Screw 2 × 4 nailing strips to the outside edges of the corner posts for attaching wallboard.

Front corner post removed for clarity

FIGURE W: Install intermediate nailing strips if the distance between the corner posts is greater than 2 ft.

A handsaw makes quick, clean work of this step if you are cutting through wallboard only **(See FIGURE T)**.

NOTE: The light shaft consists of four small stud walls that support wallboard. There is no one correct way to create the framework for the shaft, since sizes, shapes and construction obstructions and limitations vary from house to house. The steps below illustrate one solution to one specific installation. Follow along as an example, but be aware that you'll probably need to use your own creativity and knowledge of frame carpentry to construct a shaft frame that works for your skylight installation.

23 Cut pieces of 2 × 4 slightly longer than the distance from the joists above the ceiling opening to the rafters at each corner of the shaft frame area. Set a 2 × 4 at each corner and mark it for trimming to fit between the joist and the rafter **(See FIGURE U).** Cut each board to fit and toe-nail it in place. Make sure the inside face of each post is flush with the inside face of the joist. If the post is obstructed by a truss web, trim the post to fit and toe-nail it to the web. Never cut a truss member.

24 Screw 2 × 4 nailing strips to the outside edges of the corner posts for attaching drywall to the light shaft **(See FIGURE V).** Trim the nailing strips as needed to fit the full height of the shaft.

25 Install additional 2 × 4 nailing strips if the distance between the corner posts is greater than 2 ft. Miter-cut the tops as needed to fit around truss webs **(See FIGURE W).**

26 Insulate the light shaft on the attic side of the frame **(See FIGURE X).** We used loose fiberglass insulation, then stapled a 6-mil plastic vapor barrier on the inside of the shaft.

27 Attach wallboard to the insides of the shaft frame **(See FIGURE Y).** Finish the shaft with corner bead, tape and joint compound (See *Partition walls*, pages 34 to 41). Paint the shaft a light color and patch the ceiling as needed.

FIGURE X: Staple insulation on all four sides of the shaft frame. We used a loose-packed fiberglass insulation, but you can use ordinary faced or unfaced insulation batts.

FIGURE Y: Staple a 4- or 6-mil plastic vapor barrier to the inside surfaces of the light shaft frame, then cut and attach the wallboard shaft walls.

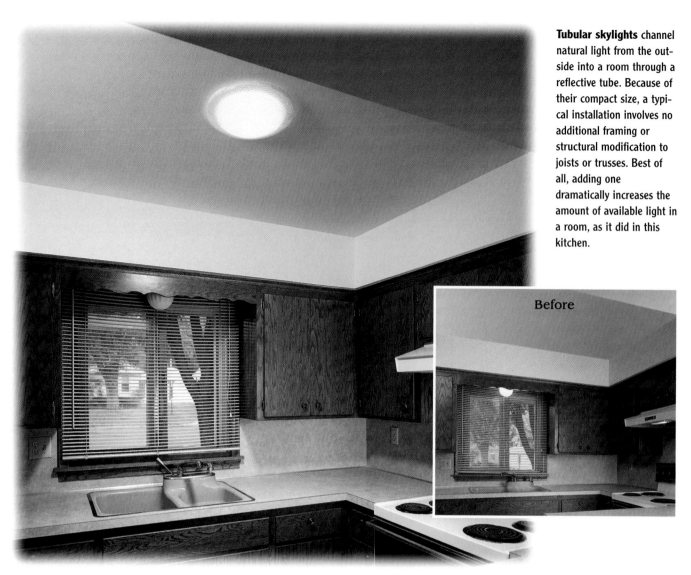

Tubular skylights channel natural light from the outside into a room through a reflective tube. Because of their compact size, a typical installation involves no additional framing or structural modification to joists or trusses. Best of all, adding one dramatically increases the amount of available light in a room, as it did in this kitchen.

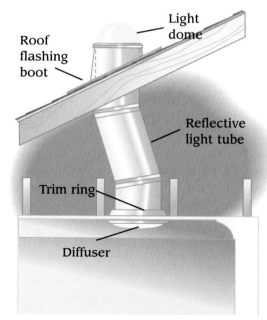

Before

Skylight variation: Tubular skylights

The tubular skylight is a close cousin to the conventional skylight. Like a skylight, it introduces natural light into a dark room. But unlike a skylight, the reflective tube that creates the "shaft" of these newer home improvement products can be twisted, bent or rerouted around obstructions in the attic area—with little or no loss of light intensity. If you've never seen one of these products in use, check one out at your local building center or home show—you'll be shocked at how much light they can bring into a room.

Tools you'll use:
In addition to the tools already listed for installing a skylight (page 85), you will need a plumb bob, jig saw and metal snips. You'll also need roofing cement to seal the flashing boot.

Light enters through a clear acrylic dome on the roof and passes through a reflective tube before diffusing into the room below. The tube can be angled as needed to accommodate the roof and ceiling framing.

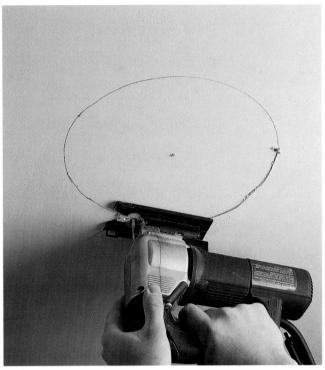

1 Select a ceiling location for the light tube that is midway between two joists and scribe a circle large enough to fit the light tube trim ring. *NOTE: You'll need to clear insulation from the joist bay first to reveal any hidden obstructions like vent stacks, ductwork or wiring.*

2 Cut the opening in the ceiling with a jig saw, following the layout line. *NOTE: If you are cutting into a textured ceiling, use a keyhole saw instead of a jig saw to minimize the damage to the textured surface.*

Starter hole

3 Hang a plumb bob from the roof sheathing above the ceiling opening. Position the bob so that it hangs in the center of the hole, and mark the end of the plumb line onto the roof sheathing.

4 Drive a screw or nail through the sheathing and shingles from inside the attic to mark the center of the light shaft on the roof. Scribe layout lines on the shingles and cut the roof section out with a jig saw. Drill a starter hole on the edge of the circle for the saw blade.

Roof flashing boot

5 Pry up the shingles around the top of the roof opening with a flat prybar and remove any shingle nails that might interfere with the metal light tube or the roof flashing boot.

6 Slip the roof flashing boot under the top shingles, center it over the opening, and outline its position on the roof. Then apply a thick bead of roofing cement around the entire area of roof covered by the flashing.

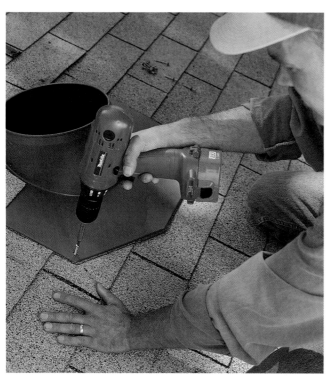

7 Seat the flashing boot into the roofing cement and fasten it in place with galvanized screws.

8 Seal the screw heads by covering them with roofing cement, then attach the plastic light dome to the flashing boot.

9 Center the trim ring in the ceiling opening and attach it with the screws provided in the tubular skylight installation kit.

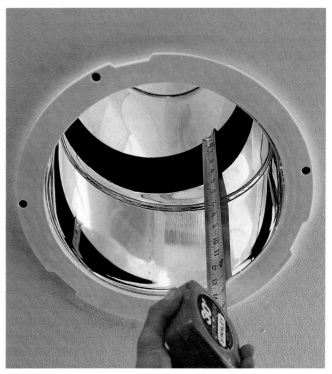

10 Attach sections of the reflective light tube to the trim ring and the roof flashing. Measure the distance (if any) that remains between the upper and lower sections of light tube.

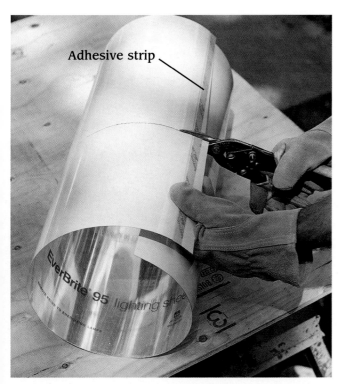

Adhesive strip

11 Cut a length of the light tube extension with a tin snips that matches the gap measured in step 10, plus enough overlap to hold the extension piece in place between the upper and lower sections of tubing. Set it into position and check the fit, then secure it by pulling off the tape that covers an adhesive strip that bonds the sides together.

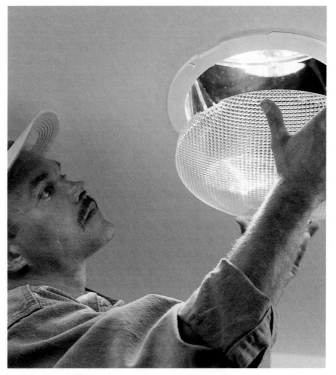

12 Snap the diffuser in place on the trim ring.

Doors

Doors create first impressions for visitors to your home. From the street, the front door is a focal point of your house, and a sturdy, fashionable entry door makes a home look more inviting and updated. As you enter the house and move from room to room, doors continue to make impressions. A gracious, smoothly operating entry door with elegant glass light panels welcomes people as they pass through it. Inside, well-chosen interior doors in good repair blend with the decor in your home to set a mood or supplement a style, while clearly and neatly dividing the living areas of your home. And there is nothing like a stately patio door to fill a home with sunlight and showcase the beauty of your backyard.

But doors aren't only about beautiful design and pleasant passages. They also provide more practical services, such as home security, energy conservation and draft reduction to make you house a more comfortable, safe and healthy dwelling place.

For one reason or another, almost every experienced handyman will need to replace or add a door in his home. Knowing the right techniques, the best tools and how to choose the perfect door for your house and budget will make your future door projects painless and highly successful.

COMMON DOOR STYLES

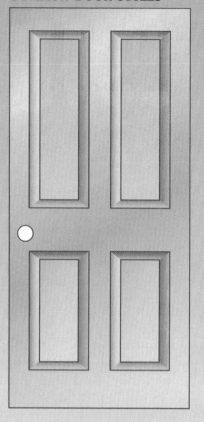

Panel door

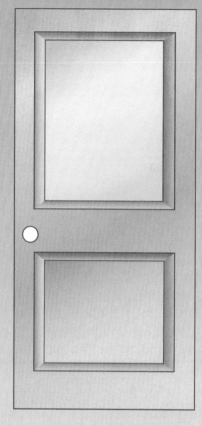

Sash door

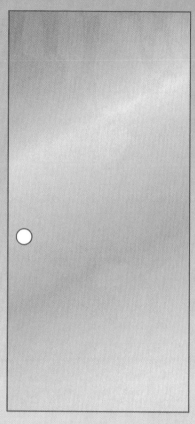

Slab door

The three most common types of doors are: *Panel doors* (left), which can have panels in many different styles and configurations; *sash doors* (middle) that feature a prominent glass panel or multi-light panel at the top; and *slab doors* (right), with flat veneered surfaces applied over a sturdy frame.

Door Basics

Hanging doors is not the painstaking process it once was. If you've ever had the experience of trying to install a heavy entry door in a hardwood jamb frame with nothing to work with but two or three sets of hinges, a handful of shims, a level and a chisel, you may have decided never to install a door again. No matter how carefully you marked and cut the hinge mortises, it didn't hang right. So you'd take the door back down, dig a little bit deeper mortise for one of the hinges and rehang the thing, only to have it be off the same amount in the opposite direction. So you'd try again. And again. And again. The process was time consuming and often very frustrating.

Today's prehung doors have eliminated most of that frustration. Whether you're installing a fancy entry door, a simple interior passage door, or a sliding patio door, the project has been simplified so even the most novice handyman can accomplish it with ease. If the new prehung door is the same size as the original, installation is as simple as removing some trim, cutting out the old door and jamb, setting the new door in the opening, shimming it, nailing it in place and reattaching the interior trim.

Despite their convenience, however, a prehung door won't fit the bill in every remodeling situation. You may find an old door that is perfect for your application but is not prehung. The layout of your house may require you to install a door that's a non-standard size. If you are a woodworker, you may prefer to build your own custom door that fits your house to a tee.

In the following pages you'll find all the information you need to accomplish any door project: from the simplest prehung passage door to custom doors and frames.

STANDARD DOOR WIDTHS

INDUSTRY NAME	WIDTH
2/0	24 in.
2/4	28 in.
2/6	30 in.
2/8	**32 in.**
3/0	**36 in.**

The most common door widths are 3/0 for exterior and 2/8 for interior. Heights are normally 80 in. (79¼ in. actual).

PARTS OF A DOOR

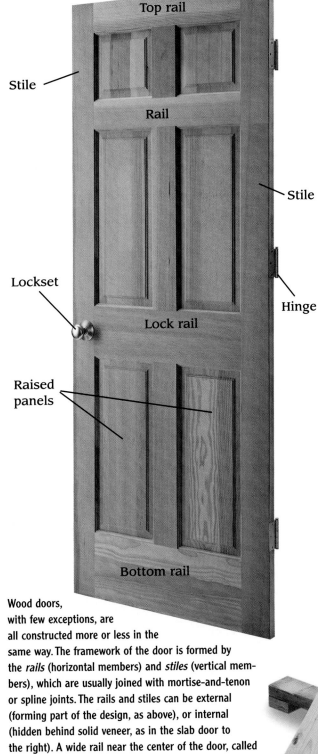

Top rail

Stile

Rail

Stile

Lockset

Hinge

Lock rail

Raised panels

Bottom rail

Right Handed:
Door pulls open
with right hand

Left Handed:
Door pulls open
with left hand

Swing direction is an important factor to consider when buying a prehung door (interior or exterior) because prehung doors are prebored for lockset installation. The easiest way to keep from confusing swing direction is to use your hands as a reminder: *Right-handed* doors are designed to pull open with your right hand, and *left-handed doors* naturally are pulled open with your left hand.

BUILD A DOOR JACK

Wood doors, with few exceptions, are all constructed more or less in the same way. The framework of the door is formed by the *rails* (horizontal members) and *stiles* (vertical members), which are usually joined with mortise-and-tenon or spline joints. The rails and stiles can be external (forming part of the design, as above), or internal (hidden behind solid veneer, as in the slab door to the right). A wide rail near the center of the door, called the *lock rail,* is designed to house the door *lockset*. On some doors, the frame is fitted with *panels,* such as raised panels with contoured edges (as above) or glass panels to create a sash door.

A door jack is a brace, usually home-made, that's designed to hold a door steady on-edge. They come in handy when planing doors for width, when cutting hinge mortises, and when sanding or finishing a door. The door jack shown here is made of plain dimension lumber.

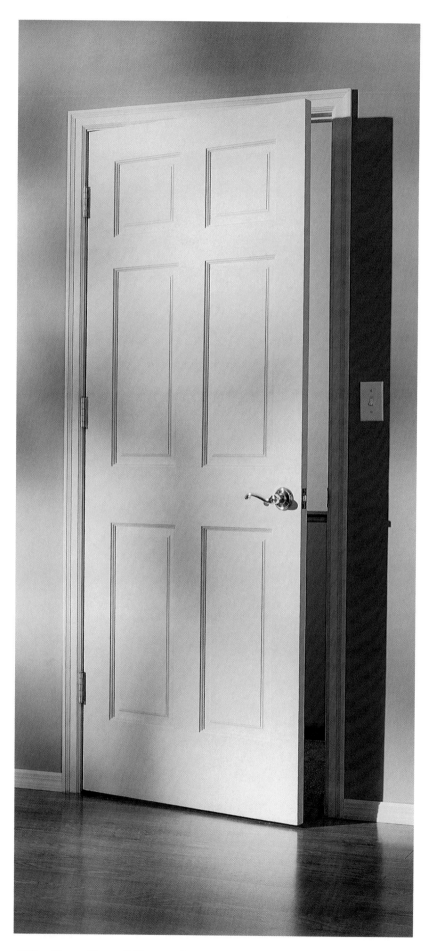

Interior Doors

Replacing a damaged or unsightly interior door is a quick and easy way to update your home. Even in older houses, door sizes are generally standardized, so in most cases you can find an interior door that will work for you at any building center.

In addition to issues of style, size and quality, the most basic decision you'll need to make when replacing an interior door is whether to choose a prehung or non-prehung door. Because they're already mounted and balanced on the door jambs, prehung doors are by far the easiest type of door to install—and consequently the most popular. New interior prehung doors almost always have hollow cores for light weight and economy, and most are slab-style, consisting of unadorned wood veneer surfaces. But installing them requires that you remove the old jambs and moldings.

If you'd prefer to leave your jambs and molding undisturbed, a non-prehung door is a better option. Remove the old door and hinges, then hang and balance a new door of the same size in the existing opening, reusing the existing hardware if you wish.

In some cases, you may find a non-prehung door that's perfect for your needs but doesn't quite fit the existing jambs. In cases like this, or if the existing jambs need replacing, you can build and install new jambs to fit the new door.

For the ultimate in custom interior doors, you can build your own door. Custom-building a door allows you to use any style or wood type you wish.

Before

Case
molding

Stop
molding

Prebored
lockset
hole

Temporary spacer

Prehung interior doors often come with case molding attached to one side of the jamb, preinstalled stop molding and prebored lockset holes for easier installation. The bottoms of the side jambs are held in place with a temporary wood spacer that must be removed before installation.

Replacing a damaged or unsightly interior prehung door is a simple remodeling project with almost instant payback.

Prehung interior doors

Most doors sold today are prehung. For both interior and exterior installation, prehung doors are shipped with the jamb and header assembled, the door fitted and hung on the hinges, and with lockset holes pre-bored (in most cases). Generally, the door trim is installed on one side of the jamb. Installing a prehung interior door involves removing the old door and jamb assembly, shimming, plumbing and securing the new door frame in the rough opening, installing the trim on the other side of the unit, and installing the lockset. Most interior prehung doors have a hollow core: Their construction consists of a lightweight internal wooden frame that supports veneered door surfaces. Solid-core interior doors are often slab style, like hollow-core doors, but the area between the veneered surfaces is filled with heavy wood or fiberglass panels.

When buying a prehung door you must know the rough opening size and the *hand* of the door (whether the door will swing to the left or right when opened—See page 101).

A

FIGURE A: Use a flat prybar to remove the case molding on both sides of the doorway. The prybar should be applied on the jamb side of the doorway to avoid damaging the walls. Use care when prying the mitered corners; they're often lock-nailed through the miter from the top (See page 107).

B

FIGURE B: Use a reciprocating saw fitted with a metal-cutting remodeler's blade to cut through the casing nails that secure the jambs and header to the wall framing members. Once all the nails are cut, pull the old jamb out of the opening.

Tools you'll use:
- Reciprocating saw with remodeler's blade (metal-cutting)
- Flat prybar
- Level
- Hammer
- Nail set
- Hand saw
- Miter saw
- Screwdriver or drill/driver
- Wood chisel

Materials list:
- Prehung door
- Wood brace (optional)
- Wood shims
- 8d casing (finish) nails
- Case molding or trim molding kit
- Wood putty
- Door lockset
- Finish materials

Installing a prehung interior door

If you've never installed a door before, installing a prehung interior door is a great way to learn the basic skills of hanging a door. Even if you're an experienced home remodeler, you'll still appreciate the ease and convenience of working with prehung doors.

1 Begin by removing the old door and jamb assembly. First, remove the hinge pins and withdraw the door from the opening. Then, use a prybar to remove the door case molding on one side **(See FIGURE A),** creating access to the void between the jambs and the wall framing members. Use care when removing the case molding—you may need to reinstall it when the new door is in place.

2 Cut the casing nails that attach the jambs to the wall framing members. A reciprocating saw with a remodeler's blade will make quick work of cutting through the nails **(See FIGURE B).** If you're having trouble spotting the nails, look for the wood shims—installers normally nail through the shims. Once the nails are cut, the old jamb assembly can be pulled out of the rough opening. This creates much less mess than trying to pry the jambs out with a prybar, and it prevents damage to the surrounding wall areas as well.

TIP: Replace spacer with a brace

Prehung doors typically come with a spacer board attached to the bottoms of the side jambs. This temporary spacer must be removed before installing the door. An easy way to keep the jamb frame square when hanging the door is to nail a piece of scrap across the jamb opening before removing the bottom spacer. Cut the brace so that it overlaps but does not extend beyond the outside faces of the jambs. Once the door is shimmed and nailed into place, remove the brace.

Nail brace to outside edges of jamb to keep door frame in square

Remove temporary spacer attached at factory

3 Remove the prehung door from the carton or wrapping and inspect the door for damage. Also remove the shipping brace that is nailed to the side jambs at the bottom of the door unit (See *TIP*, above), as well as the staples or nails driven near the lockset hole to keep the door from swinging during shipping and handling.

4 Make sure the studs in the rough opening are clear of nail ends and any other obstructions, then set the door unit into the opening. If the door unit is too tall for the opening, you'll need to trim the bottom of the door and the jambs (See *Trimming a hollow-core door*, page 108). The preattached case molding (if any) should be flush against the wall surrounding the rough opening. Slip a wood shim or two into the gap between the door unit and the wall studs. The shims will hold the door unit in rough position until permanent shims are installed and the door is attached. Use a level to check the top jamb for level **(See FIGURE C),** and to check the side jambs for plumb.

C

FIGURE C: With a few shims slipped into the gaps between the door jambs and the wall framing members, check the door unit to make sure it's level and plumb. Adjust as necessary. Also make sure preattached case molding is flush against the wall surface.

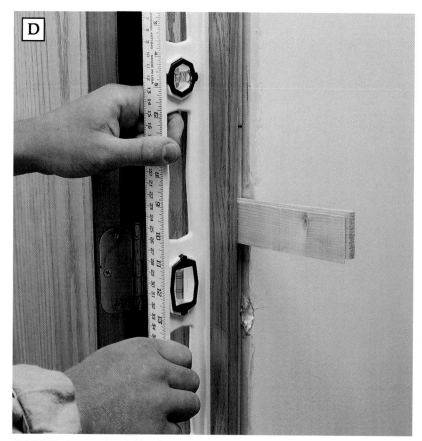

FIGURE D: Insert pairs of shims between the hinge-side jamb and the rough opening. Position them behind each hinge and adjust them in or out until the hinge-side jamb is plumb.

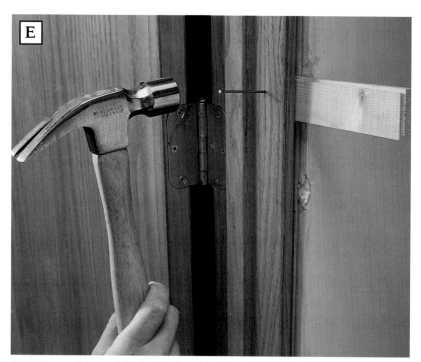

FIGURE E: Nail the jamb in place with 8d casing (finish) nails, driving them through the shims and into the jack studs at the edge of the rough opening. Then close the door and shim the lock-side jamb until a ⅛-in. gap remains between the door and lock-side jamb. Nail the lock-side jamb through the shims as well.

5 On the hinge side of the door, insert wood shims between the jack studs of the door opening and the jamb. Be sure to insert the shims so the points of the wedges face in opposite directions, forming a square unit. Position the shims behind each hinge, at the top and bottom corners and at the midpoint of the jamb. Check the jambs with a level to make sure they're plumb **(See FIGURE D).** To make adjustments, slide the shims back and forth to increase or decrease the combined thickness.

6 Move to the lockset side of the door. With the door closed, insert shims between the jack stud and the jamb at the door strike plate location. Also insert shims that are roughly level with the hinge-location shims, and additional shims at the top corner and bottom of the side jamb (aligning the shims on opposing jambs helps keep the door frame from falling out of square). For the door to close properly and for the door latch to work correctly, the gap between the jamb and the door should be about ⅛ in. thick. Adjust the shims until the lockset side of the jamb is plumb.

7 Drive 8d casing (finish) nails through the jambs and shims and into the jack studs **(See FIGURE E).** One nail per shim group is sufficient. Do not drive nails through the door stop molding.

8 After all shims are inserted and the jambs are nailed in place, use a hand saw to trim the shims so they're flush with the door jambs **(See FIGURE F).** Avoid damaging the adjoining wall surfaces with the saw.
Note: Many handymen are accustomed to breaking off the ends of the shims by striking them with a hammer. This creates several potential problems: the shim can split and fall out of the gap; the sideways pressure of the hammer blow can throw the jamb frame out of square; the ends of the shims may still protrude beyond the jambs after breakage; and there is a high risk of damage to the adjoining wall surface.

9 If your door has preattached case molding on one side, nail the trim to the jack studs and header with finish

FIGURE F: Use a handsaw to cut off the shims so they're flush with the edges of the door jambs. Hold the saw vertically when cutting to keep it from damaging the walls.

FIGURE G: Lock-nail mitered corners by drilling a pilot hole and driving a 4d nail down through the top molding and into the sides. If preattached case molding is not lock-nailed, it's a good idea to go ahead and lock-nail those pieces as well.

nails. If you have only single-layer wallboard construction, 6d finish nails should be long enough to penetrate through the trim and wallboard and into the stud. Making sure the nails hit the jack studs and door header, drive nails every 1 to 2 ft.

10 You have several options for attaching trim to the side of the door that does not have preattached case molding. Most commonly, case molding of the same profile, size and wood type is purchased then miter-cut to fit around the door opening. If you're purchasing molding to match, be sure to measure the existing molding before you go to the lumber store—you may even want to trace the profile of the case molding and bring the tracing along for reference. Make sure two of the molding strips are at least 84 in. long for the vertical frame members. When cutting the new molding strips, note that there is a reveal on the side of the door to which the trim was already attached. The reveal is the trim setback, or the distance between the inside edge of the jamb and the edge of the trim. Measure the reveal and mark the same distance for the setback on the side you are trimming. Dry-fit the trim against your reveal marks to be sure the miters match at the top corners of the trim.

11 Position the side trim along the marked reveal line. Use 4d finish nails to attach the trim to the jamb. At this point, use only a couple of nails to hold the trim in place: Do not nail the top or mitered end of the trim. Now position the trim on the opposite side of the door, and use 4d finish nails to nail the trim to the jamb. Set the head or top trim in place. Because you have not yet nailed the miter corners of the side jambs, you can adjust the miter end of the side trim slightly so the mitered corners will fit perfectly. Apply carpenter's glue to the mitered edges and nail the top trim piece in place using 4d nails to secure the trim to the jamb. At the mitered corners, predrill a pilot hole at a slight inward angle, through the top trim piece and into the side jamb trim. Drive a 4d nail through the hole to lock-nail the corners **(See FIGURE G).** If

FIGURE H: Install the door lockset assembly. The lock and bolt holes are prebored on prehung interior doors. Insert the latch bolt into the bolt hole so that the bevel side of the bolt faces the jamb. Then line up each half of the knob assembly with the bolt mechanism, and fit the knob assembly together. Secure the door lock assembly with the screws provided, according to the manufacturer's instructions.

TIP: Straightening a solid-core door

Most prehung interior doors have a hollow core, but some types are made with a solid core for greater weight and strength. Hollow-core doors are dimensionally stable, but solid-core doors may warp and develop a bow due to moisture absorption. For instance, if a door has an unequal number of paint coats on the two faces, and thus is unevenly sealed against moisture entry, the door may warp or bow toward the face that has the extra coat of paint. Often, the bow in a door may be straightened by applying an additional coat of paint or varnish to the convex face of the door. This technique is especially effective for straightening a warped cabinet or closet door.

If the door is badly warped, remove the door from the frame and position it across a pair of parallel sawhorses. The convex side of the door should face up. Lay an old blanket or other protective material on the door to protect the finish, then pile weights such as concrete blocks on the center of the door. Leave the weights in place for at least 24 hours and check the warp in the door. If the door is not straight, leave the weights in place longer. When the door is straight, remove the weights and seal the ends and edges of the door with paint or wood sealer to prevent moisture entry through the edges.

the side and top trim miters are not perfectly aligned, use a sharp chisel or sandpaper to cut away any excess so the adjoining surfaces are even. Finish nailing all the trim on the jamb side, using 4d nails. Also drive 6d casing nails into the jack studs and the rough framing header.

12 When all the nails are driven, use a nail set to drive all jamb and trim nails below the surface of the wood. With the door trim in place, install base trim and base shoe to match the existing trim. Fill the nail holes with wood putty. Stain or paint the door unit and trim to match existing trim.

13 Install the lockset. Because the lock and bolt holes are prebored on most prehung doors, lockset installation is easy. Insert the bolt assembly in the bolt hole and secure it with two screws. Do not tighten the screws until the door knob is in place. Then drive the screws that hold the two sides of the knob assembly in place **(See FIGURE H).** Tighten all screws. For more information on installing door hardware, see pages 140 to 145.

Trimming a hollow-core door

Prehung interior door units usually are made with a ½-in. gap at the bottom of the door. This gap is provided to allow the door to swing over the floor covering. For a variety of reasons you may find it necessary to cut a door at the bottom to shorten it. For example, if you install a thick carpet pad and a carpet with a high pile, the bottom edge of the door may drag against the new carpet. The only solution is to cut the door off to allow it to swing above the thicker carpet. To determine how much of the door bottom you'll need to remove, measure the distance from the floor to the top surface of the floor covering. Add ½ in. for door clearance. Subtract the distance of the door bottom from the floor as it is, and the remainder will be the amount of door you need to trim off.

On hollow-core doors, the bottom rail of the door is very narrow, and you may cut the rail off entirely when trimming the door, leaving a hollow end at the bottom. In such cases, the rail should be stripped of its veneer and reglued into the bottom of the door.

Trim the door following the step-by-step instructions on the next page.

1 Mark straight cutting lines on both sides of the bottom of the door (double-check to make sure you're working on the door bottom—it's very easy to confuse the bottom with the top) then score along the lines with a sharp utility knife, using a metal straightedge as a guide. Scoring will prevent the saw blade from splintering the veneer.

Cutting guide

2 Trim off the door bottom using a plywood-cutting blade in a circular saw. To ensure a straight cut, clamp a straightedge cutting guide to the door to guide the saw cut.

Bottom door rail

3 The cutoff portion of the door will contain the bottom door rail, which must be reinserted into the door. Scrape the veneer and any glue residue off the rail with a chisel. Then slide it back into the door.

4 Check the bottom rail for fit into the door bottom. Remove enough loose core filler material (if the door contains any) from inside the door so the bottom rail fits completely into the cavity and is flush with the door bottom. Then glue it into place with wood glue. Apply two or three padded C-clamps to hold the rail in place while the glue dries.

Custom door frames

While prehung doors are easy and convenient to install, they won't work in every home remodeling situation. Your existing door may be in fine shape, but the jamb and moldings are damaged or outdated; you might find the perfect door for your room at a salvage yard or even tucked away in a corner of your basement; or you may decide to build your own custom door to fit a non-standard opening or to match a specific design you have in mind (See *Doorbuilding*, pages 146 to 157). In any of these situations, you'll need to create your own door frame from scratch, then hang and balance the door in the new frame.

Building a custom door frame & hanging a door

Before starting, remove the old door and frame (See page 104) and measure the rough opening for the door. Subtract ½ in. from each dimension to get the correct outside dimensions for the new frame. If you're planning to use dado joints to join the header to the jambs, be sure to add back an inch into the height of each jamb.

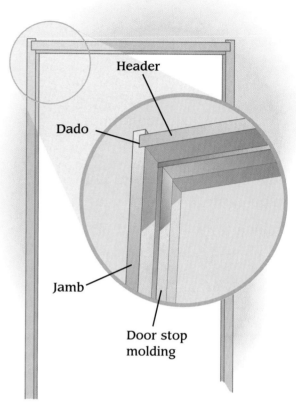

In typical door frame construction, a 1 × 6 header fits into dado or rabbet grooves at the tops of the 1 × 6 jambs. Door stop molding is added, and mortises for hinges and latch hardware are cut with a chisel.

Tools you'll use:
- Cross-cut saw
- Router
- Hammer
- Drill/driver
- Level
- Combination square
- Miter saw
- Wood chisel

Materials list:
- Door
- 1 × 6 lumber
- Wood glue
- Wood shims
- 8d casing (finish) nails
- Case molding or molding kit
- Finish materials

1 Cut the jambs and header to length from clear, straight 1 × 6 lumber. Remember to allow for the depth of the dadoes (⅜ in.) at the tops of the jambs when determining the size for the header.

2 Cut a ¾-in.-wide by ⅜-in.-deep dado at the top of each jamb to accept the ends of the jamb header. **(See FIGURE A).** We made the cuts using a router with a ¾-in. straight bit. *NOTE: The door frames on most prehung doors are made with rabbet joints at the tops of the jambs. We chose to use dado joints for greater strength and to simplify the assembly process.*

3 Glue the header into the dadoes in the jambs, and reinforce the joint with wood screws driven through the jambs and into the ends of the header. Lay the assembly on a flat surface. Use a framing square to make sure the jambs are perpendicular to the header, then attach temporary 1 × 2 cross braces at the bottom and both top corners **(See FIGURE B).**

HOW TO BUILD A FRAME & HANG A DOOR

FIGURE A: Cut ¾-in.-wide × ⅜-in.-deep dadoes in the jambs at the header height. Make the cuts in two or three passes of increasing depth. If the rough opening has a rough header in the wall framing, you'll need to use rabbet joints at the tops of the jambs, not dadoes. For speed and accuracy, gang-cut the jambs.

FIGURE B: Attach temporary braces at the corners and bottom of the frame assembly so it will stay square. The braces also ensure that the frame is flush with the wall when the assembly is pulled into the door opening.

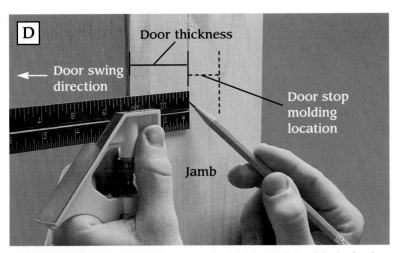

FIGURE D: Mark the door thickness on the top and side members of the jamb using a combination square and measuring in from the jamb edges on the side of the door swing direction. These reference lines mark where stop molding will be attached.

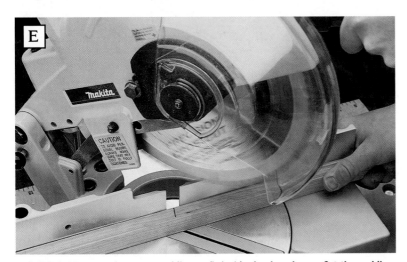

FIGURE E: Miter-cut door stop molding to fit inside the door frame. Cut the molding with the broader edge—not the molded edge—against the miter saw fence.

FIGURE C: Shim and nail the frame into place with 8d casing nails driven at the shim locations, then trim off the ends of the shims with a hand saw.

4 Set the frame into the door opening with the braces pulled flush against the wall. Install wood shims in the gaps between the jambs and the wall studs. Adjust the shims until the frame is level and plumb.

5 Drive 8d casing (finish) nails through the jambs and into the wall studs at the shim locations (you should try to locate sets of shims at hinge locations, the door strike plate locations and the tops and bottoms of the jambs). Double-check to make sure the frame is still level and plumb, then trim off the ends of the shims with a hand saw (See FIGURE C).

6 Draw reference lines on the jambs and header to mark locations for door stop molding (See FIGURE D). Miter-cut stop molding to fit the frame (See FIGURE E).

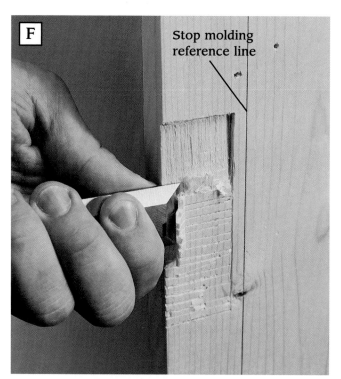

FIGURE F: Chisel hinge mortises into the jamb, leaving a ⅛- to ¼-in. setback from the stop molding reference line. Cut the outlines of the hinge leaf, then make repeated cuts across the face of the mortise about every ¼ in. Pare away the waste with the chisel (bevel facing up), working from the jamb edge across the mortise face.

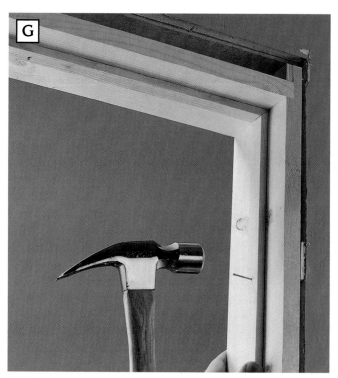

FIGURE G: Nail the stop molding in place with 4d finish nails spaced about 12 in. apart. Be sure the molding aligns with the reference lines penciled on the jamb.

FIGURE H: With the door propped up on shims and a ⅛-in. gap existing between the door and frame on all sides, mark the top and bottom of each hinge plate onto the face of the door. After removing the door, extend the marks onto the edge of the door.

FIGURE I: After cutting mortises for the hinge plates in the edge of the door, attach the hinges with one screw only and test the operation by installing the door in the door opening. If the hinges are misaligned or the door is not square in the frame, adjust the mortise depth or height to compensate until everything is aligned and working smoothly. Then attach the hinges permanently by driving all the hinge plate screws.

FIGURE J: Hang the door in the frame, then attach case molding around the door opening (See page 107).

sides. Mark the top and bottom of each hinge leaf on the face of the door **(See FIGURE H),** then remove the door to cut mortises for the hinge leaves. Pull the pins from the hinges to separate the leaves.

10 With the door in a door jack (See page 101), outline the hinge leaves on the edge of the door, using the jamb hinge leaf reference marks as guides. Cut the hinge mortises, then attach each door hinge leaf temporarily with one screw. Place the door in the opening and check the alignment of the hinge and door leaves. Adjust accordingly by trimming the hinge mortises further until the hinges align. When all the hinges align and the door swings and closes properly, secure the door hinge leaves with screws **(See FIGURE I).**

11 Hang the door in the frame, using shims underneath for support **(See FIGURE J).** Install the hinge pins and check the gap between the door and the jamb—it should be about ⅛ in. and equal around the door. Attach case molding and paint or stain the door as desired. Install the rest of the door hardware (See pages 140 to 145).

7 Lay out hinge locations on the door jamb. For interior doors, two 3-in. butt hinges are usually enough to hold the door. The top of the upper hinge should be about 9 in. down from the header. The bottom of the lower hinge should be about 10 in. up from the floor. If you add a third hinge, center it between the upper and lower hinges. The depth of the mortise should equal the thickness of a hinge leaf. The mortises should start ⅛ to ¼ in. outside the stop molding reference line. Outline the hinge leaves at the correct locations, and remove waste wood with a chisel **(See FIGURE F).**

8 Nail the door stop molding in place with 4d finish nails at 12-in. intervals along the molding reference lines **(See FIGURE G).**

9 Attach the hinges to the jamb and set the door in place. Check to see that a ⅛-in. gap exists around the door on all

Trim out the door and apply your finish of choice before installing the lockset and door latch to complete the project.

Ideal for situations where door swing is obstructed or unwanted, pocket doors slide into a frame inside the wall cavity when the door is opened, as this "X-ray" photo reveals.

Pocket doors

Pocket doors are popular in high traffic areas and in closets or bathrooms where there is little room for a hinged door to swing open. To install a pocket door, you'll need to remove the wall coverings and framing members next to the door opening. If the wall area next to the door you're hoping to replace with a pocket door is occupied by a window or another door, you're out of luck. Doors next to plumbing or ductwork are not well suited for pocket doors either because of the difficulty of rerouting these obstructions. Wiring can usually be rerouted fairly easily if you're set on retrofitting a pocket door. If you're building a new partition wall, be sure to plan for the pocket door frame.

Pocket doors fit into preassembled frames, usually made of thin rails and stiles to fit inside the wall cavity. Some frames have protective metal on the frame members so wallboard screws and other fasteners can't be driven into the frame opening, where they'll damage the door. It's possible to find pocket door kits that include both the door and the frame. But as likely as not, you'll end up buying the door separately. Slab-style hollow-core doors are generally used for pocket door installations, since heavier doors will cause too much strain on the overhead tracks that support the door. The pocket door installation sequence on the following pages is fairly typical, but specific hardware and methods vary by manufacturer. Read the instructions for your door unit carefully before you start.

Tools you'll use:
- Utility knife
- Flat prybar
- Reciprocating saw
- Level
- Drill/driver
- Hammer
- Nail set
- Miter saw
- Table saw
- Wood chisel

Materials list:
- Pocket door frame
- Slab-style hollow-core door
- Wood shims
- Wallboard and finishing supplies
- Wallboard screws
- Dimension lumber and case molding
- 4d finish nails
- Pocket door latch and pulls

Installing a pocket door

Before beginning a pocket door installation project, remove the old door and trim moldings. Also remove any base moldings and crown moldings in the vicinity of the project area. Inspect the area where the frame will be installed for any signs of wiring, plumbing or ductwork. Shut off electrical power to the work area at your main service panel.

1 Measure out from the existing door opening to outline the area of wall covering you'll need to remove to install the pocket frame. This distance should equal the width of the door plus 4 to 6 in. At this distance, scribe a straight vertical line on the wall surface from floor to ceiling. Score along the line with a utility knife—this helps prevent damage to the surrounding wall area when wall coverings are removed **(See FIGURE A)**. Remove wall coverings above the door opening.

2 Pry off the wallboard or plaster in the project area. Once you've removed a small section of wall covering, inspect the wall cavity for any hidden obstructions. Continue removing the wall covering until the entire project area is revealed **(See FIGURE B)**. Remove the coverings on the other side of the wall in the same manner. *NOTE: On lath-and-plaster walls, remove the plaster first, then use a circular or reciprocating saw to cut through the lath around the project area. Remove the lath. Be careful that you do not cut through hidden wiring.*

HOW TO INSTALL A POCKET DOOR

FIGURE A: Mark out the project area on the wall adjoining the door opening, then score along the outline from floor to ceiling with a utility knife.

FIGURE B: Pry off the wall coverings in the project area, keeping a lookout for any obstructions in the wall cavity. Dispose of waste promptly to keep the work area clear.

3 If the project wall is load-bearing (See page 44), provide temporary support before beginning the removal of any wall framing members. If you are unsure if the wall is load-bearing, check with your local building inspector.

4 Cut through the framing members in the project area, including the king stud and jack stud at the

FIGURE C: Cut the wall studs in the project area in half with a reciprocating saw, then pull or pry them free from the cap plate and sole plate.

TIP: Flip the recip saw blade to cut sole plates

To make flush cuts with a reciprocating saw, install the blade so the teeth face up toward the top of the saw, then cut with the saw turned upside down.

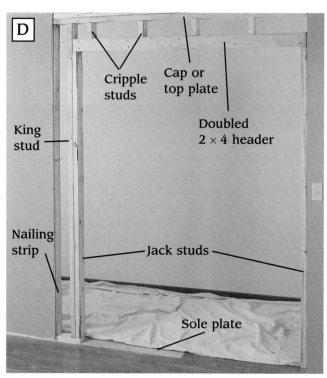

FIGURE D: Install framing members to create the rough opening for the pocket door. In addition to the new king stud, jack stud, cripple studs and header, you'll need to replace the jack stud on the non-frame side of the door opening with a new stud that supports the doubled 2 × 4 header. Also add 2 × 4 nailing strips behind the edges of the wall coverings to create nailing strips.

Cripple studs

Cap or top plate

Doubled 2 × 4 header

King stud

Nailing strip

Jack studs

Sole plate

edge of the door rough opening, using a reciprocating saw. Remove the cut studs **(See FIGURE C).**

5 Frame the rough opening according to the pocket door manufacturer's instructions for the size of the door you're installing. You'll be adding a new door header, cripple studs and jack and king studs **(See FIGURE D).** If needed, install a stud to provide nailing surfaces for the wallcoverings.

6 Cut the sole plate flush with the inside face of the jack stud and remove it (See *TIP,* above).

7 Position the pocket door frame in the opening **(See FIGURE E)** and shim around it until it's plumb and level. Attach the frame to the jack stud with 16d common nails or 3-in. deck screws driven every 12 to 18 in.

8 Slide the door track into place inside the top of the door frame **(See FIGURE F).**

9 Shim the door track as needed to level it at the proper height **(See FIGURE G).** Attach the track at shim locations with wallboard screws driven into the 2 x 4 rough header.

10 Screw wallboard to the new framing members and to the pocket door frame **(See FIGURE H).**

FIGURE E: Set the pocket door frame into the opening, making sure to keep the open end on the side of the door opening.

FIGURE F: Set the sliding door track into rough position at the top of the door frame.

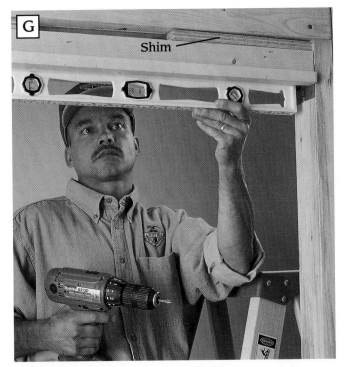

FIGURE G: Use a level to make sure the door track does not slope. Insert shims between the track and the door header to correct any problems. Attach the track with screws driven up into the header. Then check the rest of the frame for plumb again and screw it to the rough opening every 12 in.

CAUTION: Make sure screws used to attach wallboard do not break through the inside faces of the frame rails, causing the points to scratch the door.

FIGURE H: Patch over the frame area with new wallboard or plaster attached to the framing members and the horizontal rails of the pocket door frame. Use wallboard screws, not nails.

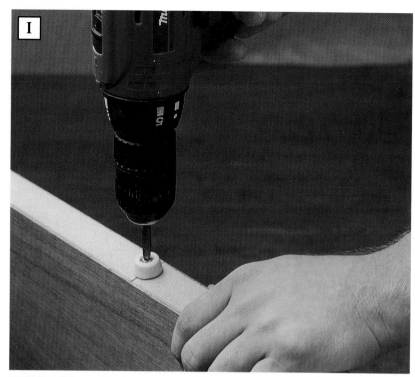

FIGURE I: Select a slab door that fits the height and width requirements of the opening and pocket door frame. Screw the rubber door bumper to the edge of the door that recesses into the pocket door frame. This will soften and quiet the impact of the door in its frame when the door is opened.

FIGURE J: Attach door hanger hardware with the screws provided to the top of the slab door approximately 4 in. from either door edge.

11 Select a slab-style door that fits the height and width requirements of the door opening and pocket door frame. Screw the rubber door bumper (provided with the door frame) to the edge of the door that leads into the door frame **(See FIGURE I).**

12 Attach the door hangers to the top of the door, about 4 in. from each end of the door **(See FIGURE J).**

13 Hang the door by sliding the door hangers onto the runners in the overhead door track **(See FIGURE K).** Work with the hardware until the door fits properly in the frame and travels smoothly. Once you've installed trim around the door jambs and opening, removing the door becomes more difficult. If you haven't applied a finish to the door yet, now is a good time.

14 With the pocket door installed and recessed in the frame, begin trimming out the door opening. Because the exact dimensions of trim you'll need can vary, you may have difficulty locating exactly the right pieces of millwork. But you can easily rip-cut the pieces you'll need on a table saw. In addition to a jamb on the open side of the door opening, you'll want to cut trim strips to conceal the ends of the door frame. Also attach door stop molding to the overhead track and the new jamb to conceal hardware and fashion a recess for the door when it's closed. Attach the trim with 4d finish nails **(See FIGURE L).**

15 Trim around the door opening with miter-cut case molding. Attach plastic tracking guides to the bottom of the trim pieces at the opening into the frame area **(See FIGURE M).** These guides keep the door from rocking as it moves back and forth.

16 Install recessed door pulls and a pocket door latch, according to the hardware manufacturer's directions **(See FIGURE N).** Most standard door hardware is not designed for use with pocket doors.

FIGURE K: Slide the track runners into the door hangers and clip them in place. Test the door operation on the track and adjust as necessary until the door travels smoothly and recesses completely into the wall.

FIGURE L: Cut and install a new jamb on the open edge of the door opening. Attach door stop molding to the undersides of the overhead track and to the jamb to create a recess area for the door when closed. You may need to rip-cut these trim parts on your table saw to fit. Also attach trim to cover the exposed edges of the door frame.

FIGURE M: Attach case molding around the perimeter of the door opening on each side of the doorway. Install and adjust the plastic door guides that keep the bottom of the door tracking properly.

FIGURE N: Install the recessed door pulls and latch hardware, according to the manufacturer's directions.

Exterior Doors

Exterior doors create a transition between your home and the rest of the world. They provide protection as well as access; they offer welcome along with security; they are the primary focal points to the outside of your home as seen by everyone else.

Advancing technology has had a great impact on the basic construction of exterior doors. Most exterior doors sold today are fabricated with cores made of fiberglass or high-tech wood products that provide insulation against heat and sound exchange, while resisting expansion and contraction caused by changes in temperature and humidity. The shells of newer exterior doors are made from a variety of material. Steel-shell doors are perhaps the most common today because they offer durability and strength at relatively low cost, and the manufacturers have developed the ability to make steel look warm and inviting.

The majority of entry doors being made today feature some kind of light panel—usually made with double-insulated, reinforced glass. Concern over break-ins has led designers to locate the light panels higher and higher on the door over recent years, making it more difficult for intruders to smash the glass, then reach in and unlock the door from the inside.

Even patio doors, which are primarily glass, have advanced technologically in past years. Exterior patio doors often feature double-insulated glass panels, the tracking devices are designed to make break-ins more difficult, and new security aids seem to come on the market every year. The latest technological advance, which is also occurring in the windows market, is to enclose mini-blinds between the glass patio door panels. The blinds are still easy to open and close, but because they are encased, they never get dirty and they're unlikely to become tangled or damaged.

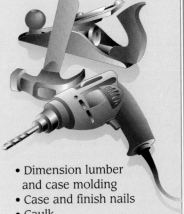

Before

Entry doors

Replacing an entry door can refresh the curb appeal of your home and bring immediate energy savings to your household budget. Most entry doors sold today are 36 in. wide (32 in. wide is also a standard size), and they come in an extraordinarily wide range of prices. For ease of installation, choose a prehung door.

Installing a prehung entry door

Installing a prehung exterior door is similar to installing a prehung interior door. Read the section on hangingprehung interior doors (pages 104 to 108) for additional information you may find useful when installing an exterior door.

Tools you'll use:
- Utility knife
- Flat prybar
- Reciprocating saw
- Level
- Drill/driver
- Hammer
- Nail set
- Miter saw
- Wood chisel

Materials list:
- Entry door
- Wood shims
- Deck screws
- Dimension lumber and case molding
- Case and finish nails
- Caulk

A

FIGURE A: Remove the old door. Hollow-core doors, like the one above, can be managed by one person, but for most doors it's a good idea to get a helper to keep the door from falling and causing damage.

B

FIGURE B: Remove the case molding from around the door frame to create access to the jambs. Handle the case molding carefully if you plan to reuse it.

1 With your old entry door closed, tap out the hinge pins with a hammer and screwdriver. Remove the door **(See FIGURE A).**

2 Remove the case molding around the jamb with a flat prybar **(See FIGURE B).** For tightly fitting molding, or in cases where you plan to reuse the trim, slice and pry with a putty knife or paint scraper first to create a gap between the jamb and the molding.

3 Remove the old threshold **(See FIGURE C).** In older homes, the threshold is probably nailed to the door sill and can be pried out. But if the threshold contains a rubber strip running lengthwise along the center, remove the rubber strip before attempting to pry out the threshold—the strip often conceals screws used to anchor the threshold. Remove all screws.

4 Cut through the casing nails that attach the jamb to the wall studs using a reciprocating saw with a metal-cutting or remodeler's blade **(See FIGURE D).**

5 Pull the old jamb out of the opening from outside the doorway **(See FIGURE E).** On older doors the sill may be fastened to the bottoms of the jambs and will need to removed along with the jambs.

6 Inspect the sill for rot or other forms of damage. If it is in good condition and the new door doesn't come with a sill attached, reuse the old one (you may want to give it a quick coat of primer or sealant while you have the chance). Fasten the sill to the subfloor with deck screws **(See FIGURE F).** If you need to replace the sill, use the old sill as a template if possible and cut the new sill from pressure-treated lumber (a 2 × 6 will work on most newer homes). Sills in older houses tend to be thinner.

7 Make sure the framing members for the rough opening are free of nails, then set the new door unit into the rough opening and test the fit of the door and the brick mold. The brick mold (preattached on most prehung doors) should be tight against the surrounding sheathing—not overlapping the siding. The gaps between the brick mold and the edges of the siding

should be no more than ⅛ in. If the brick mold does overlap the siding, trace around the brick mold with a pencil and remove the siding in the outlined area (See page 64). If your home has stucco or masonry siding, you'll probably find it easier to remove the brick mold, rip it to fit, then reattach it to the door frame. If the gaps are wider than ⅛ in., either replace the brick mold with wider molding, or rip-cut filler strips and glue them to the preattached brick mold before final installation of the door unit. *Note: Because the door shown in this project butts up against the soffit on the exterior side, there is no need to install drip cap at the top of the door opening. But if the top of your door will butt up against siding, cut a strip of drip cap to fit the width of the opening, apply panel adhesive to the back edge and slip it between the wall sheathing and the siding. Do not use nails or screws to attach drip cap. If the existing drip cap is in good condition, leave it in place.*

8 Once the door opening is adjusted to fit the door and brick mold, apply a bead of caulk or panel adhesive to the back of the brick mold and to the surface of the door sill, then set the door unit back into the rough opening **(See FIGURE G)**.

9 From inside the house, insert pairs of wood shims into the gaps between the door unit and the wall studs. Shims should be inserted at hinge and lockset locations and approximately every 12 in. along the jambs. Adjust the shims until the side jambs are plumb and the header is level. Drive 10d galvanized casing nails at each shim location, through the jambs and into the wall framing members. **(See FIGURE H)**.

10 Fasten the brick mold to the wall framing with 10d casing nails, spaced 12 in. apart **(See FIGURE I)**. Set the nail heads and cover with wood putty.

11 Adjust the threshold height to fit against the bottom of the door **(See FIGURE J)**. Most new prehung exterior doors come with a preinstalled threshold that can be height-adjusted by turning adjustment screws beneath the rubber strip in the center.

12 For security, replace one or two of the hinge screws on the jamb-side leaf of each hinge with 3-in.-long screws that penetrate into the wall studs **(See FIGURE K)**.

13 Trim off the ends of the shims, then insulate the gap around the jambs (See page 138). Attach case moldings **(See FIGURE L)** and door hardware (See page 140). Paint or finish the door and moldings to match, using exterior-rated products. Apply caulk around the brick mold and the threshold.

FIGURE C: Peel the old rubber door seal out of the grooves on top of the threshold and check for screws. Remove the old threshold.

FIGURE D: Cut through the casing nails that attach the door jambs to the wall studs using a reciprocating saw with a remodeler's blade.

FIGURE E: Remove the old door jamb assembly. Then clean up the rough opening by removing any old shims or nails that might interfere with the new installation.

FIGURE F: Inspect the sill and replace it if needed. The sill shown above was in good condition, but we recoated it with primer/sealant since we had the chance. Drive a few deck screws to cinch the sill in place.

FIGURE G: Apply caulk or panel adhesive to the back sides of the brickmold and to the top of the sill, then set the new door unit into the rough opening.

FIGURE H: Shim between the jambs and the jack studs until the door is square in the opening, then secure the door with casing nails driven through shim locations.

FIGURE I: Attach the brickmold to the wall studs with 10d galvanized casing nails. Make sure to keep the nails centered side to side so the brickmold doesn't split.

FIGURE J: Adjust the threshold height so the bottom of the door just brushes the threshold when it closes. The threshold shown above has built-in height adjustment screws.

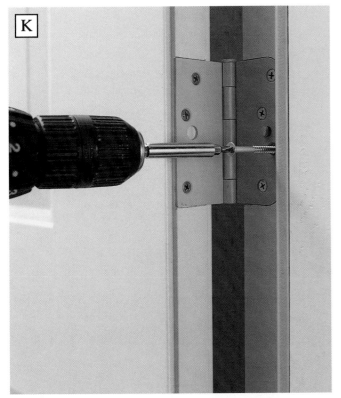

FIGURE K: Replace one or two of the short hinge screws provided by the door manufacturer with 3-in. wood screws. The longer screws will penetrate all the way through the jamb and into the jack stud.

FIGURE L: Reinstall the door case molding, or cut new molding to fit. Attach the case molding with 6d finish nails driven into the front edges of the jack studs and header.

Patio Doors

Perhaps more than any other home feature, patio doors effectively bring the outdoors into your home. Patio door glass area alone is double or triple the size of most windows and extends nearly from floor to ceiling. Yet today's glass technology and door design don't sacrifice comfort or energy dollars for a larger view. The popularity of patio doors means there is an array of styles and configurations to choose from to match nearly any home and budget.

The photos on this page show just how dramatic the transformation can be when you replace an ordinary wood entry door with a new patio door. The room becomes brighter and takes on an open feeling. Access to outdoor living spaces like decks or porches is improved. And the two areas become connected in a way that makes both the indoor and outdoor spaces feel larger and more complete.

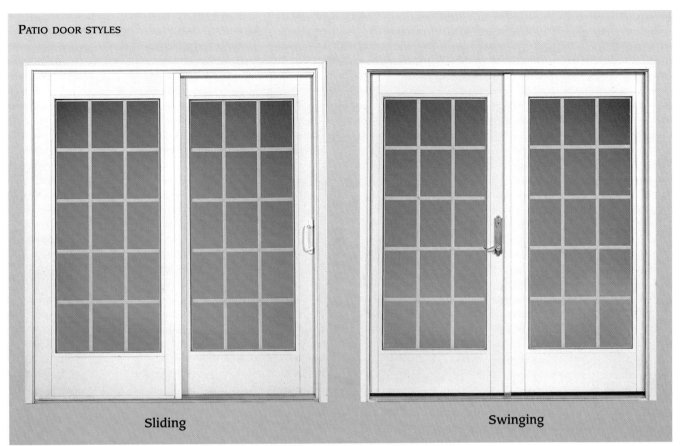

Sliding

Swinging

When selecting a patio door, a basic choice you'll need to make is whether you want a door with sliding glass panels or one with panels that swing open and shut. *Sliding patio doors* are a good choice if you plan to leave the door open for long periods of time to create ventilation, or if either side of the door is a high traffic area or likely to be obstructed. One other advantage to sliding doors is that both panels can be removed from the tracks to allow clear access to the full door opening. *Swinging patio doors* are generally more energy efficient and less prone to water leakage than sliding doors, and they pose less of a security risk. But the permanent jamb between the glass panels can get in the way when moving large objects in and out of the house, and the hinged doors are vulnerable to damage when left open.

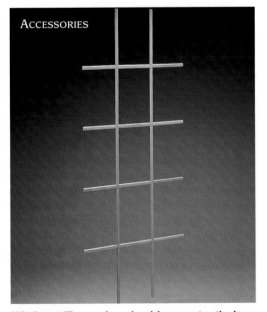

ACCESSORIES

Window grilles can be ordered from most patio door manufacturers. Overlaid on the glass panels, they fit into the door frame in one piece to create a French door appearance.

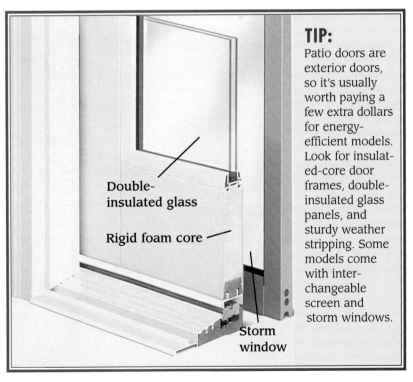

Double-insulated glass

Rigid foam core

Storm window

TIP:
Patio doors are exterior doors, so it's usually worth paying a few extra dollars for energy-efficient models. Look for insulated-core door frames, double-insulated glass panels, and sturdy weather stripping. Some models come with interchangeable screen and storm windows.

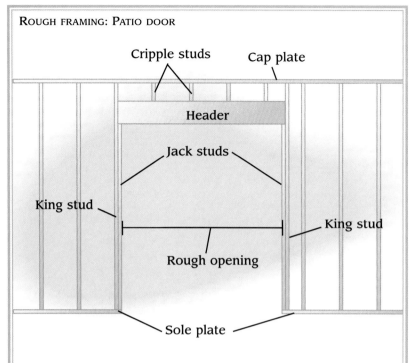

Cripple studs   Cap plate

Header

Jack studs

King stud

King stud

Rough opening

Sole plate

The rough framing for a patio door is similar to the framing for any other door. Due to the width of the rough opening, however, a wide header made from built-up dimension lumber or even engineered beam material is often required. Before starting a patio door installation project, make sure that the required header is not so wide that the rough opening becomes too short for the patio door.

Installing a patio door

Installing a patio door is similar to other door installation projects. But because the doors are extra wide, you'll likely encounter door header support issues, and the chances are good that you'll need to reroute some wiring to make room for your new door. Unless you're replacing an old patio door,

Tools you'll use:
- Reciprocating saw
- Utility knife
- Flat prybar
- Level
- Drill/driver
- Hammer
- Nail set
- Miter saw
- Table saw
- Wood chisel

Materials list:
- Patio door
- Wood shims
- Wallboard for patching
- Wallboard screws
- Dimension lumber and case molding
- 4d finish nails
- Brickmold
- Construction adhesive and caulk

Security Tip

Keyed patio door lock

Security bar

Patio door pin

Patio doors, especially sliding patio doors, can be inviting entry points for uninvited guests. But there are several products you can buy to increase the security of your patio door. A *keyed patio door lock* attaches to the frame of a fixed door panel, at the top or bottom of the panel. The bolt at the top of the device slides into a hole in the door frame or threshold, where it prevents the door panel from sliding. The bolt requires a key to be retracted. A *security bar* fits into the door track to prevent the sliding door panel from moving. Commercial models can be telescoped for a tight fit; or you can simply cut a piece of 2 × 2 to fit snugly between the sliding panel and the jamb. A *patio door pin* also is designed for use with sliding patio doors. This simple device relies on the same principle as other window sash pins. A hole is drilled through the frame of the inside panel and part-way into the frame of the outside panel. A small escutcheon is inserted into the hole. When the door is closed, the holes in the door frames will align and can be held together by inserting the pin.

HOW TO INSTALL A PATIO DOOR

FIGURE A: Provide temporary support before removing any structural members from a bearing wall—a temporary stud wall about 4 ft. longer than the project area is shown here (See page 13).

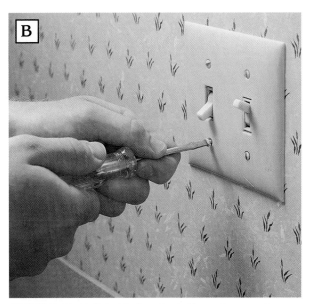

FIGURE B: Shut off electrical service to the work area and remove switch and receptacle plates, wall and door trim, and other obstructions mounted to the wall.

FIGURE C: Remove the old door, then cut the fasteners holding the old door jamb to the wall studs using a reciprocating saw (See page 104). Remove the old jamb assembly and threshold.

installing a patio door will require a building permit. You must have your plan approved before beginning the work.

1 Install temporary support. We built a temporary stud wall with a double header, positioned about 3 ft. away from, and parallel to, the wall containing the door opening **(See FIGURE A)**.

2 Shut off electricity to the work area at the service panel. Remove switch and cover plates, as well as door trim and base moldings in the work area **(See FIGURE B)**.

3 Remove the old door, jamb frame and threshold **(See FIGURE C)**.

4 Outline the rough opening for the door on the wall surfaces. The instructions for the door unit you purchase will list the required rough opening size (usually about 1 in. larger than the outside dimensions of the door unit). In most cases, you can minimize the amount of framing you'll need to do by keeping the existing king stud on one

FIGURE D: Mark layout lines on your interior wall for the patio door rough opening—the lines should be exactly vertical, extending from the floor to the ceiling.

FIGURE E: Carefully remove the wall coverings in the project area. Working in small sections is the safest way to strip the wall without causing damage to the area surrounding the rough opening.

side of the old door opening. Use a level to draw outlines all the way from floor to ceiling—you'll need to completely remove the framing members in the work area **(See FIGURE D).** Score along the outlines with a utility knife so the wall covering will break off cleanly. If possible, adjust cutting lines so they fall over the next framing member outside the work area. This will allow you to patch in with new wall covering later without the need to install additional framing members to use as nailing surfaces.

5 Remove the wall covering in the outlined work area by prying off one section, then pulling or prying the rest free **(See FIGURE E).** If you use a flat prybar to pry pieces off, be careful around wiring and any other wall components. Once the wall surface is removed, dispose of the debris immediately. Pull away the plastic vapor barrier and remove the insulation.

6 Remove wiring or other obstructions in the wall section to be removed **(See FIGURE F).** If you're not experienced working with the mechanical systems like wiring or ductwork in your house, hire a professional to perform this phase of the remodeling project. If you're comfortable working with these systems (and you know what you're doing!), involve your building inspector from the outset. In most areas, a separate inspection of any electrical or plumbing work is required. Don't be tempted to cut corners on this part of the project—in addition to the safety hazards, you may end up having to undo your work and even pay fines if the proper procedures aren't followed. Make sure all wires are capped and secured well outside of the work area.

7 Remove wall framing members in the work area **(See FIGURE G).** Take care to avoid damaging the cap plate and the wall sheathing adjacent to the

project area. Cut stubborn studs in the middle with a reciprocating saw, then remove them in two pieces, pulling or hammering the sections loose.

8 Re-route wiring and other wall elements outside of the project area. Install any outlets or wall switch boxes in their new positions **(See FIGURE H).** Once the rough-in of these systems is completed, contact your local building department to arrange for an inspection, if required. *NOTE: If you hire a certified contractor to make changes to any of your mechanical systems, the contractor generally will take care of obtaining permits and arranging for inspections.*

9 Cut a new king stud to fit between the sole plate and the cap plate at the side of the new door rough opening (If you've removed both original king studs, install two new ones). Many handymen routinely cut retrofit wall studs slightly too long for the opening so the tension when they're driven into position will hold them in place. It's okay to add an ⅛ in. or so to the length, but don't add any more than that. A stud that's too long can bow or cause the studs directly next to it to loosen at the tops. Set the king stud in position and check with a level to make sure it's plumb. Then mark the king stud locations on the cap plate and sole plate. Toe-nail the king stud into position with 10d common nails—don't forget to allow for the jack stud that will be nailed to the side of the king stud that faces the rough opening.

10 Subtract the width of the door header from the height of the king stud, and cut two new jack studs to that length (you can try to salvage the old jack stud at the original side of the rough opening by trimming off the top to allow for the new header, but you're probably better off removing and replacing both jack studs). Face-nail the jack studs to the king studs with 10d nails **(See FIGURE I).**

11 Construct the new door header (See page 13). In the project shown here, a pair of 2 × 10s sandwiched around ½-in. plywood would have had enough strength to bear the load. But the height

FIGURE F: Disconnecting and rerouting wires and other wall components is a job best left to professionals. But if you choose to do the work yourself, be sure to include the information in your permit application so the building inspectors can approve your plan and examine your work.

FIGURE G: Remove the framing members in the rough opening area.

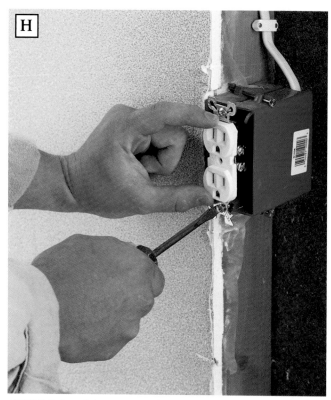

FIGURE H: Install (or arrange to have installed) boxes for receptacles or light switches, according to your remodeling plan.

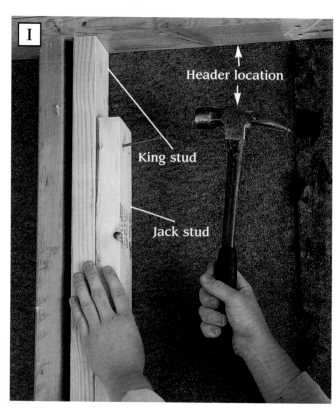

FIGURE I: Face-nail jack studs to king studs to create the borders of the rough opening. Be sure to leave the correct amount of space for the door header.

FIGURE J: Install the door header. The one shown here is made from engineered beams for extra strength.

FIGURE K: With the saw blade inverted in your reciprocating saw, cut through the sheathing and exterior siding (if wood lap siding), then cut through and remove the sole plate.

FIGURE L: With a helper, tip the patio door unit into place in the rough opening. Removing one or both doors beforehand will make this easier to do. Keep in mind that you'll need to remove the door again before final installation.

of the door unit we planned to install didn't leave enough room for a 9¼-in.-wide header. So we consulted with the local building inspector and used an engineered beam instead of dimensional pine to make the header. The engineered beam was strong enough to bear the weight, while occupying less space. So we rip-cut two pieces of the beam to the maximum width that could fit into the opening. Then we nailed the header beam in place by driving 10d nails through the king stud and into the end of the beam on the open side of the opening. We toe-nailed the beam to the jack stud on the other side of the rough opening, then toe-nailed up into the cap plate in several spots **(See FIGURE J).**

12 Cut the opening into the exterior wall. The

Note:
In the project shown here, the patio door area is covered by a roof and not exposed to the elements, so no drip cap was needed above the top of the door opening. If your door will be exposed, install drip cap between the siding and the sheathing before you install your door.

house shown here is sided with wood lap siding, so we simply were able to follow along the edges of the rough opening, cutting from inside with a reciprocating saw and remodeler's blade. If your house has metal, vinyl or masonry-based siding, see the *TIP* on the following page.

13 Cut through and remove the sole plate at the edge of the rough opening to make room for the new door threshold. To accomplish this, turn the blade in your reciprocating saw around so the teeth are flush with the top of the saw **(See FIGURE K).**

14 Clear out any debris from the rough opening area, such as old wood shims, that might interfere with the installation. The threshold area needs to be level with the adjoining subfloor, so you may need to do some patching. In our project, we used concrete to fill in a void left by the old threshold.

15 Unpackage the door unit and test-fit it in the opening **(See FIGURE L).** To make the unit easier to handle, we removed the sliding door panel (even

FIGURE M: Use a piece of brickmold (or preattached brickmold on some doors) as a spacer to outline the trim area on the siding.

FIGURE N: Remove the door unit and cut along the siding trim lines with a circular saw. Finish the cuts with a hand saw.

TIP: Removing exterior siding

Wood lap siding is the easiest type of siding to cut out and remove. In most instances, you can simply cut through it with a reciprocating saw. This technique can be used with vinyl, steel and aluminum siding, provided you use a metal-cutting blade. But the preferred method is to remove the siding in the project area, cut through the sheathing, then trim each piece of siding and replace it as you go.

If your house has stucco or masonry veneer siding, you've got a much bigger project on your hands. To remove stucco, insert a masonry bit in your drill and drill out through the rough opening at the corners. Push a nail through the hole at each corner, then snap chalklines on the stucco between the nails. Score along the outline with a masonry chisel, then cut along the outline from outside, using a circular saw and masonry-cutting blade. Finish the cuts with a masonry chisel, then knock out the stucco. Cut through the wire lath base with a reciprocating saw or metal snips. Brick veneer siding must be disassembled—a job for a professional.

then, two workers were needed to prop the unit up into the opening). Level the unit in the opening, using strips of treated plywood as shims, if necessary. Do not attach the door unit to the framing members yet.

16 With the door unit leveled and positioned so the gap between the unit and the rough opening is even on both sides, mark the exterior siding for trimming. Trimming around the opening allows the brick mold to fit flush against the wall sheathing (brick mold is not meant to overlay siding). If your door unit has preattached brick mold, simply trace around the perimeter with a pencil to mark the siding. If it has no brick mold attached, use a piece of the brick mold you plan to use as a spacer and trace around the door on the sides and top **(See FIGURE M).**

17 Remove the door unit from the opening. Trim back the siding to allow for the brick mold, using a circular saw **(See FIGURE N).** Finish the cuts at the corners and bottoms with a hand saw, then remove the siding in the brick mold area. The cutting depth of the saw should be just slightly greater than the thick-

FIGURE O: Gaps between the sill area of the door opening and decks or steps can be bridged with transition strips.

Nailing fin

FIGURE P: Apply panel adhesive or caulk to the threshold and to the nailing fins (or brickmold) before installing the door unit.

ness of the siding to keep the sheathing intact.

18 Install transition pieces as needed to bridge any gaps between an existing deck or set of steps and the threshold area of the door. In our project, we filled in with a thin strip of decking **(See FIGURE O)**.

19 Prepare to install the door unit. To create a good seal, apply beads of exterior panel adhesive around the sill area and along the inside faces of the nailing fins (or the backside of preattached brick mold) on the new door frame **(See FIGURE P)**.

20 Replace the door in the rough opening so the nailing fins (or brick mold) are flush against the exterior sheathing. Install pairs of shims every 12 in. around the jamb, and shim from below with strips of treated plywood, if necessary, to bring the door unit to level. Check the side jambs with a level to see if the door is plumb, and adjust the shims **(See FIGURE Q)**.

21 Drive one or two galvanized deck screws through each nailing fin and into the wall fram-

ing members to tack the door in position. Doors with preattached brick mold should be secured by driving 16d galvanized casing nails through the brick mold and into the framing members. If you removed one or both of the door panels, reinstall them and test to make sure the doors operate properly. If not, adjust the shims until the doors track smoothly. Then, remove the door panels again for protection and finish securing the door unit by driving screws or nailing around the frame at 8- to 12-in. intervals **(See FIGURE R)**.

22 If your door did not come with preattached brick mold, cut side strips and a top strip of brick mold to frame the door. Miter-cut the joining ends at 45°. *TIP: If the brick mold you purchase is unfinished, apply primer to all surfaces before you install it. This will help protect the brick mold from water damage and rot.*

23 Apply panel adhesive or caulk to the backs of the brick mold strips, and attach them in a frame around the door. Use galvanized 8d casing nails driven every 12 in. or so **(See FIGURE S)**.

FIGURE Q: Use pairs of wood shims to adjust the door unit until it's plumb in the opening.

FIGURE R: Tack the door unit in place with a few nails or screws so you can test the operation of sliding doors before securing the door unit for good.

24 Reinstall the sliding door panel. It should operate smoothly in its tracks and form a clean joint with the other door panel when closed **(See FIGURE T).**

25 Apply a bead of paintable, siliconized latex caulk around the perimeter of the door where the brick mold meets the siding **(See FIGURE U).** Fill all nail holes with caulk. Lay a bead of caulk at the point where the sill meets the threshold of the door as well.

26 Most sliding patio doors have an adjustment screw located on the bottom of the sliding door frame, on the edge that butts up against the door jamb when the door is closed. Tighten or loosen the adjustment screw **(See FIGURE V)** until the door closes evenly against the jamb—there should be no visible gap anywhere, from top to bottom, along the joint.

27 Inside the house, trim the shims flush with the inside edges of the jambs, using a hand saw.

28 Pack the voids between the rough opening and the door unit with fiberglass insulation **(See FIGURE W).** Be sure to wear protective eyewear, a particle mask and work gloves when handling fiberglass insulation. Do not overpack the insulation—if it's compressed too tightly, its insulating value is reduced.

29 Patch around the new door with wallboard (See pages 34 to 41). If the edge of the opening in the wall doesn't fall over a framing member, install a 2 × 4 nailing strip so the wallboard edge is centered on the nailer. The edges of the wallboard patches should butt up against the outer faces of the door jambs **(See FIGURE X).** Use care when driving drywall screws

FIGURE S: Frame the door with miter-cut brickmold attached with construction adhesive and casing nails.

FIGURE T: Make a final test of the operation of sliding door panels to make sure everything works smoothly.

FIGURE U: Caulk the gap between the brickmold and the siding with paintable caulk.

Tracking adjustment screw

FIGURE V: To micro-adjust the tracking of the sliding door panels, most new patio doors feature an adjustment screw. Tighten or loosen the screw until the sliding door closes perfectly against the door jamb.

FIGURE W: Fill the gaps between the door and the rough opening with fiberglass insulation to cut down on drafts and heat transfer. Don't overpack the insulation.

FIGURE X: Measure, cut and install wallboard on the inside wall around the patio door. The edges of the wallboard should butt up against the outer faces of the door jambs.

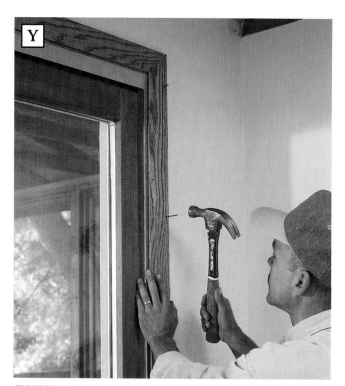

FIGURE Y: Trim around the inside perimeter of the door as you would any other door with case molding that's finished to match the rest of the woodwork in the room. Drive the nails below the wood surface with a nailset and cover the holes with tinted wood putty.

FIGURE Z: A narrow gap between the new door threshold and the floor is typical. There's no single correct way to conceal the gap, but a thin strip of wood used as a transition does a good job.

around electrical wiring. Tape and coat the seams with three coats of drywall compound. Sand and finish the wall with primer and paint or wallpaper, then reinstall the outlet and switch covers.

30 Miter-cut and install case molding around the inside door frame with 6d finish nails **(See FIGURE Y).** To avoid messing up the newly painted or papered wall surfaces, pre-stain or paint the trim to match your existing woodwork. If your new patio door is unfinished on the interior, also stain and top-coat (or paint) the door frame to match your woodwork. Reinstall the base molding and any other wood trim to the walls. Drive the nails below the surface with a nailset and cover the holes with wood putty.

31 In some installations, you'll end up with a narrow gap between the inside of the door threshold and the finished floor. Simply cover the gap with a narrow strip of transition molding attached to the floor with construction adhesive and 8d finish nails **(See FIGURE Z).**

32 As a finishing touch, we purchased and installed a pair of wooden window grille kits (See *TIP,* above). Then we added a supplementary patio door lock (See page 128) for extra security.

TIP: Window grilles

Among the more appealing patio door accessories you can purchase are pre-fabricated window grilles that create the appearance of a French door. Sold as a kit with hardware by many patio door manufacturers, these grilles simply snap into place with the use of small bullet clips. Window screens and other accessories can also be purchased separately. Unlike most doors, patio doors usually include door pulls and locks that are preinstalled.

Because the project turned out so well and privacy was not a concern in the backyard of this house, we elected not to install blinds or curtains on our patio door. If you'd prefer more privacy from outside, look for a door with integral mini-blinds installed between the glass panes.

Door Hardware

Once you've gone through the effort of carefully completing the installation of your new door, the final step is to install the door hardware, including a knobset or lockset, a deadbolt lock for exterior doors, and any miscellaneous types of hardware for specific applications. Installing the hardware carefully and correctly has a direct impact on how successfully the new door fulfills its purpose, as does making good choices when selecting the hardware to be installed.

Just as doors are designed either for interior or exterior purposes, most door hardware is better suited for use with one type or the other.

Interior door hardware. There are two basic types of interior door *locksets* (the assembly including the doorknobs, the cylinder connecting them inside the door, the latch bolt, and the strike plate for the latch bolt). The most common is the *passage lock.* This lock has a knob on each side of the door and is used where privacy is not a concern. The second type of interior door lock is the *privacy lock.* With a locking knob operated by a thumbscrew or push button on the inside knob, the privacy lock is used on bathroom doors and sometimes on bedroom doors. Supplementary locks, like deadbolts, generally aren't used on interior doors.

Knob

Escutcheon

Connecting screw

Spindle

Latch bolt faceplate

Latch bolt

Cylinder

Most door locksets sold today have similar working components. The knobs (which may or may not contain a locking mechanism) are drawn together by a pair of connecting screws that run through the cylinder. Inside the cylinder, a spindle turned by each knob is connected to a latch bolt. The latch bolt extends and retracts according to which direction the knob is turned, causing it to engage or disengage from the recess in the strike plate mounted in the door jamb.

Deadbolt locks

Prehung exterior doors today usually come predrilled to accept a deadbolt lock above the lockset. Deadbolts provide significantly more protection against door kick-ins than the lockset because the lock bolt extends deeper into the door jamb. If any of your exterior doors currently are not fitted with a deadbolt, adding one would be a wise security measure.

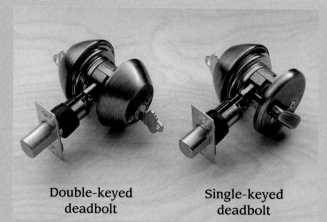

Double-keyed deadbolt

Single-keyed deadbolt

Deadbolt locks most commonly have a keyed knob on the exterior side and a thumb-turned lock on the interior knob (called a single-keyed deadbolt). But double-keyed deadbolts are becoming increasingly popular, especially on doors with light panels, to prevent intruders from reaching in and unlocking the deadbolt.

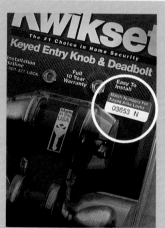

Key coding information lets you buy a lockset and deadbolt that can be operated with the same key. You can also have locks re-keyed to match by a locksmith.

Designer door hardware

The door hardware sections at most building centers are large, but as you examine the products closely, you'll find that there are really only a handful of choices that will work for your door. This is especially true of doorknobs and plates, the bulk of which come in only two basic shapes and three metal choices: brass, antique brass or brushed steel. If you're looking for something a little fancier or for hardware to match your existing older door hardware, check at a building materials salvage yard or locate a reproduction hardware catalog (you can usually find several of these catalogs, along with toll-free telephone numbers, listed in home renovation magazines).

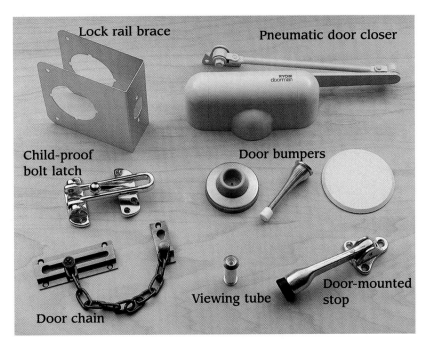

Miscellaneous door hardware is installed on an as-needed basis, usually to address security concerns or to protect the door and the adjoining wall from damage.

Because most interior doors have a great enough swing radius to contact the wall when fully opened, a *door bumper* is normally mounted to the baseboard in the area where the door meets the wall. *Hinges* are preinstalled on prehung interior doors. When installing a non-prehung door, two 2½- or 3-in. butt hinges with removable hinge pins typically are used.

Exterior door hardware. Locksets for exterior doors generally are somewhat heavier than those for interior doors, and they always include a keyed lock. Deadbolt locks are installed as a standard practice today. Other types of hardware for exterior doors include *door chains, door closers, viewing tubes, door stops* or *bumpers,* and various security enhancement devices. Exterior doors generally are hung on three 2½- or 3-in. butt hinges of slightly heavier gauge than interior door hinges. Exterior doors also require a threshold that creates a seal between the sill plate on your house and the bottom of the door. Because they endure so much wear, thresholds require occasional replacement (if not the entire unit, then at least the rubber threshold top strip).

Specialty door hardware. Less common door types, like sliding patio doors and pocket doors, require specialty hardware. See the sections of this book discussing these types for more information.

Door locksets come in three basic types: *passage locksets* (sometimes called *knobsets*) commonly found on hall, closet and bedroom doors; *privacy locksets* installed on bathroom and bedroom doors; and *keyed entry locksets,* used mostly on exterior doors.

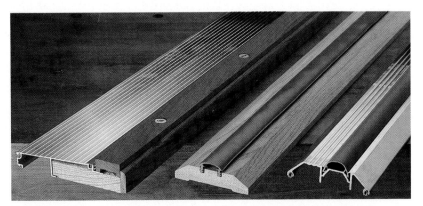

Door thresholds are usually preinstalled on prehung exterior doors, but frequently installers choose to replace them with different models that blend in closer to the house style, fit the existing space better, or contain more efficient sealing strips. Look for a threshold that matches the old threshold as closely as possible in size, shape and style.

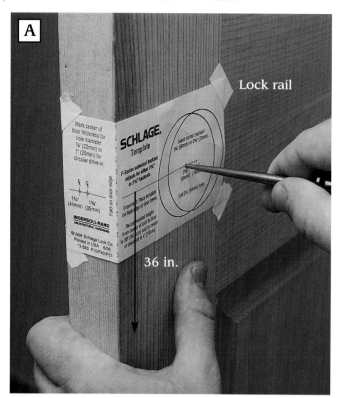

FIGURE A: Tape the drilling template provided by the lockset manufacturer around the edge of the door in the correct position, then mark centerpoints for drilling the lockset cylinder hole and the latch bolt hole.

FIGURE B: Use a hole saw to drill out the lockset cylinder hole. Drill through from one side until the guide bit breaks through the opposite face of the door, then finish drilling the hole from that side.

How to install a door lockset

Because prehung doors usually have predrilled holes for the door lockset (and sometimes the deadbolt on exterior doors), installing a lockset is a quick and simple process. If the door you've installed is not pre-bored, you'll need to drill holes for the lockset cylinder and the latch bolt, as well as mortise out a recess in the jamb for the latch strike plate. To help guarantee a proper installation, most lockset manufacturers provide a full-scale drilling template you attach directly to the door. Read the lockset manufacturer's instructions before you start. If your door is predrilled, skip ahead to *step 4* in the following sequence.

1 Position the drilling template (if one was provided with your lockset) around the non-hinged door edge so the centerpoint of the lockset hole is at the correct height (36 in. up from the door bottom is standard). Most drilling templates are laid out to be used with either an interior (1⅜-in.-thick) or exterior (1¾-in.-thick) door. Make sure to use the markings corresponding to the thickness of the door you've installed. Tape the drilling template to the door and check the height on both sides of the door. Use a scratch awl or nail to mark the centerpoints for drilling the lockset hole and the latch bolt hole **(See FIGURE A).** If you

Tools you'll use:
- Utility knife
- Drill/driver
- Hole saw
- ⅞-in. spade bit
- Wood chisel
- Screwdriver

Materials list:
- Door lockset (Knobs, cylinder, latch bolt and strike plate)
- Wood screws

don't have a drilling guide for your lockset, you'll need to measure in from the edge of the door to find the centerpoint of the cylinder hole. The best way to find the correct distance is to preassemble your lockset and latch bolt and measure the distance from the middle of the spindle that fits into the latch bolt to the point where the end of the latch bolt begins to taper. Then, with the door closed, measure out that amount from the edge of the door stop molding and mark the drilling point on both sides of the door.

2 Use a hole saw of the size listed in your lockset instructions (in some cases, hole saws are included

in the package with the lockset) to bore out the cylinder hole **(See FIGURE B).** Taking care to keep the drill perpendicular to the door, drill through one side of the door until the hole saw guide bit punches through the other side. Then remove the hole saw and complete the cylinder hole from the opposite side of the door using the guide hole as a reference. *TIP: If you're installing a metal-clad exterior door, use a twist bit the same thickness as the guide bit for the hole saw to predrill all the way through the door.*

3 Bore the latch bolt hole from the edge of the door through to the cylinder hole, using a spade bit **(See FIGURE C).** Most latch bolts require a 7⁄8-in.-dia. bit, but there are exceptions, so be sure to check the instructions. Keep the drill perpendicular to the door edge while boring the hole. If you're working alone, brace the open door on each side with a heavy weight to help keep it from swaying as you work.

4 Insert the latch bolt in the latch bolt hole (the tapered end should face the door jamb) and outline the latch bolt faceplate on the edge of the door, making sure the latch bolt is level **(See FIGURE D).** Remove the latch bolt and score along the edges of the outline with a utility knife. Remove the wood in the outline area with a wood chisel until the recess is equal in depth to the thickness of the faceplate.

5 Insert the faceplate in the recess and mark drilling points for screw pilot holes (or, if you have a vix bit the correct size, use it to drill the pilot holes). Drill pilot holes for the faceplate screws, then insert the latch bolt assembly and screw the faceplate securely to the door.

6 Install the lockset. One of the knobs will have guide holes for the screws that draw the two halves of the lockset together. The faceplate, or *escutcheon,* for the other knob is free of guide holes—this knob should be installed on the outside of exterior doors. Insert the knob into the hole so the spindle attached to the knob fits through the hole near the end of the latch bolt **(See FIGURE E).** Insert the

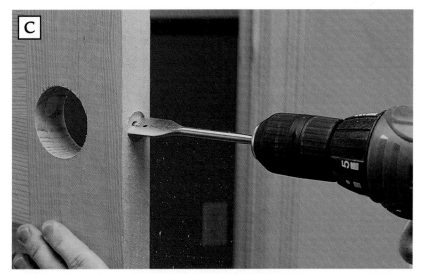

FIGURE C: Bore the latch bolt hole from the edge of the door through to the cylinder hole with a 7⁄8-in. spade bit. Keep the drill perpendicular to the door.

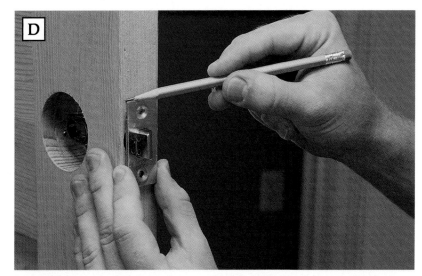

FIGURE D: Insert the latch bolt and outline the latch bolt faceplate onto the edge of the door to create an outline for mortising the door to accept the faceplate.

FIGURE E: Insert the knob assemblies into the cylinder hole so the spindle fits through the latch bolt and into the other knob and the connecting screws align.

FIGURE F: With the door closed far enough that the latch bolt meets the door jamb, mark the location of the top and bottom of the latch bolt onto the door jamb. Then, with the door open, transfer the reference lines to the inside face of the jamb to use as guides for drilling the guide hole for the latch bolt into the jamb.

Inside edge of door

FIGURE G: To locate the correct position of the latch bolt guide hole, first measure the distance from the inside edge of the door (the edge that contacts the stop molding on the door jamb) to the flat edge of the latch bolt.

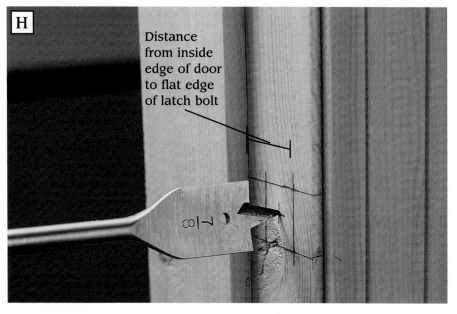

Distance from inside edge of door to flat edge of latch bolt

FIGURE H: Use your reference lines and measurements to outline a box representing the area where the latch bolt will strike the door jamb. Find the center of the box and drill through the jamb to create a guide hole that accepts the latch bolt when the door is closed.

other knob assembly into the hole so the spindle fits into the knob and the connecting screws inserted into the escutcheon are aligned with the screw holes on the inside of the other knob. Press the two knob assemblies together. If you're installing a door with a handle instead of a knob, make sure the handle is in a horizontal position and the latch bolt is fully extended. Tighten the connecting screws to draw the two knob assemblies together.

7 Close the door far enough so that the latch bolt touches the door jamb, then mark the top and bottom edges of the latch bolt where it crosses the jamb **(See FIGURE F).** These marks will serve as reference points for positioning the strike plate. Extend the lines across the face of the jamb.

8 Measure the position of the latch bolt in the door to determine where to drill the guide hole for the latch bolt in the jamb **(See FIGURE G).** The key distance is from the inside edge of the door (the edge that contacts the stop molding) to the flat edge of the latch bolt. Also measure the thickness of the latch bolt.

9 Measure out from the stop molding and mark the jamb where the flat surface of the latch bolt will fall. Measure back from the line and mark the thickness of the latch bolt. Extend the points to form a box with the reference lines marking the top and bottom of the latch bolt. Find the center of the box and use it as a centerpoint for drilling a guide hole for the latch bolt **(See FIGURE H).** Drill the hole. The guide hole should extend all the way through the jamb.

10 Close the door and check the fit of the latch bolt. If it doesn't fit cleanly, use a file or rasp attachment mounted in your drill to pare the hole until the latch bolt fits in smoothly **(See FIGURE I).** Keep the hole as small as possible so it will be covered by the strike plate.

11 Outline the strike plate on the jamb, then cut a mortise as you did for the latch bolt face plate (Steps 4 and 5). Install the strike plate **(See FIGURE J).**

FIGURE I: If you find that you need to enlarge the guide hole slightly to accept the latch bolt cleanly, try using a rasp attachment (inset photo) mounted in your power drill.

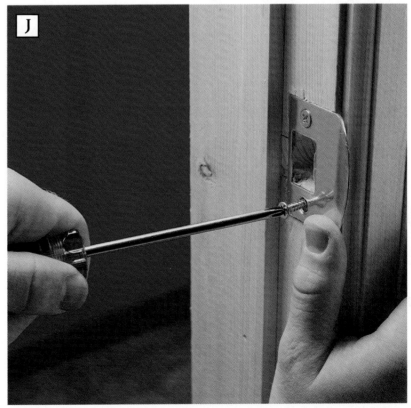

FIGURE J: Attach the strike plate to the jamb. The mortise for the strike plate should be just deep enough that the metal plate is flush with the surface of the wood.

Before

Doorbuilding

Even with the wide variety of doors you can buy off the floor or custom-order from manufacturers, you may want to consider building your own custom door. By building it yourself, you can match surrounding wood materials and styles, you can add a unique feature, like the light panel in the door above, that you might not be able to find even in custom doors. But most of all, by building a door yourself you can ensure that the craftsmanship and materials combine to create a door that will last for the lifetime of your home.

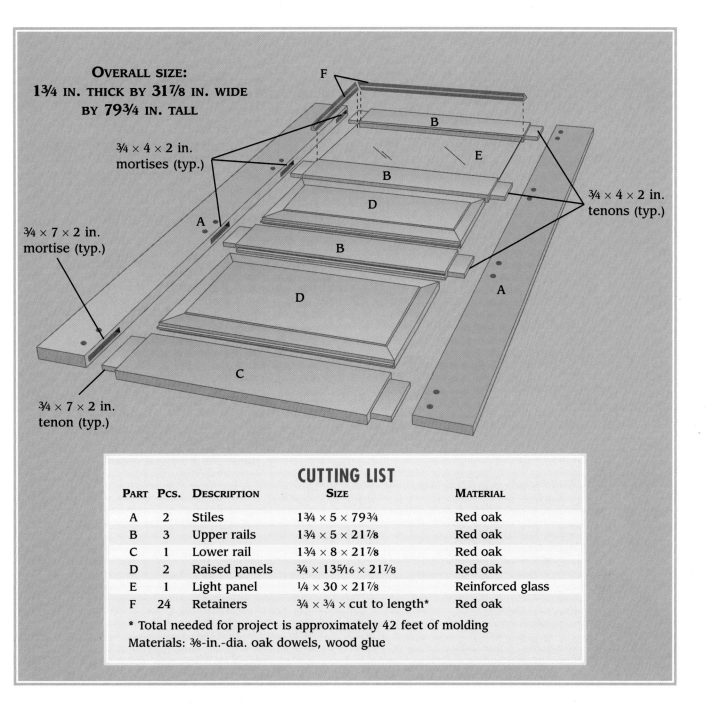

OVERALL SIZE:
1¾ IN. THICK BY 31⅞ IN. WIDE
BY 79¾ IN. TALL

¾ × 4 × 2 in.
mortises (typ.)

¾ × 7 × 2 in.
mortise (typ.)

¾ × 4 × 2 in.
tenons (typ.)

¾ × 7 × 2 in.
tenon (typ.)

F

B

B

E

D

B

D

A

A

C

CUTTING LIST

Part	Pcs.	Description	Size	Material
A	2	Stiles	1¾ × 5 × 79¾	Red oak
B	3	Upper rails	1¾ × 5 × 21⅞	Red oak
C	1	Lower rail	1¾ × 8 × 21⅞	Red oak
D	2	Raised panels	¾ × 13 5/16 × 21⅞	Red oak
E	1	Light panel	¼ × 30 × 21⅞	Reinforced glass
F	24	Retainers	¾ × ¾ × cut to length*	Red oak

* Total needed for project is approximately 42 feet of molding
Materials: ⅜-in.-dia. oak dowels, wood glue

Building your own door can be a gratifying project that offers a great opportunity to show off your woodworking skills and your creativity. A finely crafted, handmade door makes a dramatic statement that improves the character of any room. But if you live in a colder climate, you should be aware that building an exterior door from solid wood may create problems. Today's exterior doors usually are made from solid-core materials like wood composite or fiberglass. These materials provide good insulation and, more importantly, they resist movement much better than solid wood. A solid wood door can expand or contract in size by as much as 5 to 15%, which can cause it to

stick in the door frame in warmer months, and to become drafty and poorly sealed in winter months. Even in warm, stable climates, you're probably better off focusing your talents and energy on interior door projects.

The door shown in this chapter, for example, was designed to replace a solid raised-panel door leading into a small entry area. Here, the front entry door absorbs the temperature changes. The door we built has a large light panel to brighten the entry area by allowing light from the house into the area. And on warmer days, it allows natural light into the house if the front door is opened.

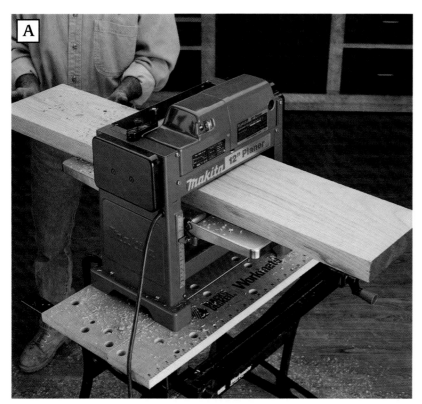

FIGURE A: Plane both faces of the door rail and stile stock so the finished workpieces are 1¾ in. thick.

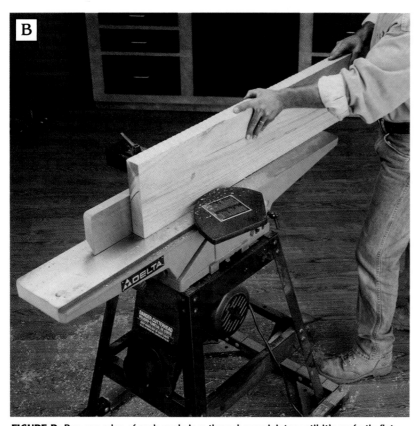

FIGURE B: Run one edge of each workpiece through your jointer until it's perfectly flat, even, and square to the planed face.

Tools you'll use:
- Table saw
- Tenon jig
- Planer
- Jointer
- Miter saw
- Drill/driver
- Drill guide
- Router
- C-clamps
- Pipe clamps
- Wood chisel

Materials list:
- Door lumber (See *Cutting list*, page 147)
- ⅜-in. oak dowels
- 1-in. wire brads
- Wood glue
- Reinforced glass
- Finishing materials

Building a raised panel door

Made of solid red oak, this raised-panel door features an expansive light panel that brightens a dark entryway and also allows sunlight into the house when the front entry door is opened. The rails and stiles are connected with mortise-and-tenon joints. The oak panels are shaped around the borders with a table saw to create a traditional raised-panel relief. The panels fit into grooves in the rail and stile frames. Because we made this door with full ¾ oak, its finished thickness is a hefty 1¾ in., and the finished door weighs in at over 100 pounds. Because of the weight, we added a third hinge to hang the new door.

1 Fully work out your door plan. Before you begin building, make sure you have a detailed drawing showing dimensions, joinery and fasteners; a thorough cutting list with number of parts, materials, and finished dimensions recorded; a shopping list for purchasing lumber and other materials; and an efficient plan, including assembly steps, for building the door.

• Make the rails & stiles •

2 Begin by preparing the wood stock for the rails and stiles. Plane the faces of

FIGURE C: Rip-cut rails and stiles on the table saw with the square edge of each piece of stock against the fence. Cut the pieces so they're oversized by 1/16 in. Run the sawn edges over the jointer to bring stiles and rails to finished width.

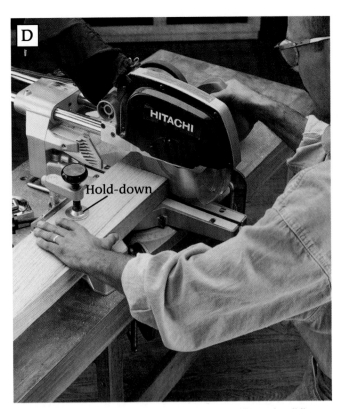

FIGURE D: Cross-cut the rails and stiles to length. We used a sliding compound miter saw. Be sure to use the hold-down clamp on power miter saws.

all boards at the same time, running each face through your surface planer before changing the thickness setting. We planed all the wood stock until the boards were each exactly 1¾ in. thick **(See FIGURE A).**

3 Run one edge of each board over the jointer to create a square, flat edge **(See FIGURE B).** Now that you have adjoining faces that are flat and square to one another, you can rip-cut the boards to width on your table saw or band saw. *TIP: For greatest accuracy control, rip the board slightly (about 1/16 in.) wider than called for, then trim it to finished width on your jointer.* Be sure the jointed edge of each board rides against the saw fence **(See FIGURE C).** Note that in the plan shown here the bottom rail is wider than the rest of the rails.

4 Cross-cut the rails and stiles to length **(See FIGURE D).** We used a power miter saw, but a table saw, radial arm saw or circular saw and straightedge cutting guide could also be used.

• Cut the mortise-and-tenon joints •

5 The door rails are joined to the stiles with mortise-and-tenon joints—a common method for assembling the framework of a door. For lighter doors, butt

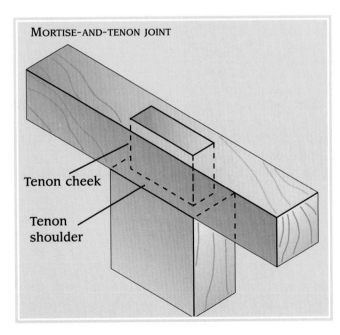

joints reinforced with dowels, splines or even biscuits may be used. But for maximum strength and resistance to joint failure, the mortise-and-tenon is hard to beat. We started by cutting the tenons at the ends of the rails. Our plan calls for tenons that are 2 in. long and ¾ in. thick, starting ½ in. from the top and bottom edge of each rail. We used a shop-built tenoning

Construction diagram: Table saw tenoning jig

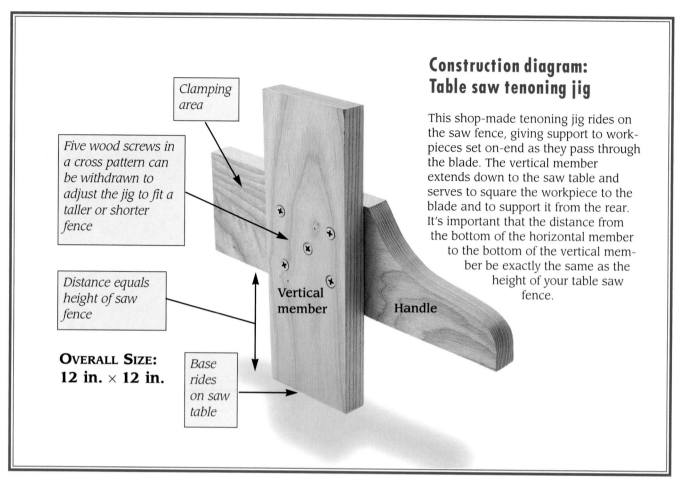

Clamping area

Five wood screws in a cross pattern can be withdrawn to adjust the jig to fit a taller or shorter fence

Distance equals height of saw fence

OVERALL SIZE: 12 in. × 12 in.

Base rides on saw table

Vertical member

Handle

This shop-made tenoning jig rides on the saw fence, giving support to workpieces set on-end as they pass through the blade. The vertical member extends down to the saw table and serves to square the workpiece to the blade and to support it from the rear. It's important that the distance from the bottom of the horizontal member to the bottom of the vertical member be exactly the same as the height of your table saw fence.

E

Tenoning jig

FIGURE E: Make the cheek cuts for all tenons using your table saw and a tenoning jig. Clamp each rail securely against the vertical member of the tenoning jig before making the cuts. On the same end, flip the workpiece and cut the other cheek. Repeat cutting these cheeks on both ends of all the rails.

jig **(See Construction diagram, above)** as a guide for making the deep cheek cuts in the rail tenons. To make the cheek cuts, clamp the workpiece to the tenoning jig with the table saw fence ½ in. from the blade. Raise the blade height to 2 in. Clamp a rail securely against the vertical member of the tenoning jig and make the cheek cut. On the same end, flip the workpiece and cut the other cheek. Repeat cutting these cheeks on both ends of all the rails **(See FIGURE E).**

6 To make the shoulder cuts on the tenons, first clamp a relief block to the table saw fence on the infeed side of the blade, well back from the point where the workpiece will contact the blade. With an auxiliary fence attached to the miter gauge, use the relief block to set the distance of the end of the workpiece from the saw blade. Set the blade height to the depth of the cut needed to remove the correct amount of wood (½ in. for the door shown here). Make the shoulder cuts on all four sides of each tenon **(See FIGURE F).**

FIGURE F: Clamp a relief block to the table saw fence on the infeed side of the blade. Set the fence so that the stock, butted against the relief block, will pass over the blade and cut the shoulders in the rail tenons. Using the miter gauge, cut the shoulders for each rail tenon.

Relief block

Auxiliary miter gauge fence

7 Lay out the mortises for all joints on the inside edges of the door stiles. To ensure that the mortises align, gang-mark the top and bottom of each mortise with the stiles clamped together edge-to-edge. The bottoms of the lower three mortises should be the following distances from the bottoms of the stiles: ½ in., 21¹³⁄₁₆ in., and 40⅛ in. The mortises for the top rail should be ½ in. down from the tops of the stiles. Use a combination square to mark the top and bottom of each mortise across the faces of the stiles **(See FIGURE G).**

8 Outline the mortises on the edges of the stiles. Position the tenons over the outlines to make sure the mortises are the correct sizes. To cut the mortises, we used a drill and ¾-in.-dia. Forstner bit mounted in a right-angle drill guide to remove most of the wood in the mortise area (the drill guide ensures that the bit remains perpendicular to the drilling surface). *SAFETY TIP: Never use a Forstner bit in a portable drill without a stable drill guide.*

FIGURE G: Line up the ends of both stiles and mark the mortise locations using a combination square. Ganging both stiles together helps ensure that the mortises will align.

FIGURE H: Remove most of the waste wood from the mortises by drilling overlapping holes with a Forstner bit and drill mounted in a portable right-angle drill guide.

FIGURE I: Square and clean up the walls of each mortise with a sharp chisel. The beveled edge of the chisel should face into the center of the mortise.

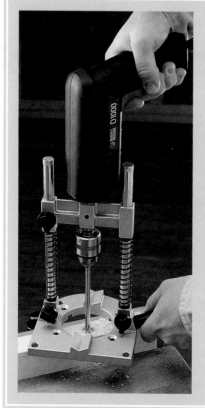

Portable drill guides

A drill guide lets you use a portable power drill in many of the same ways you'd use a drill press. By mounting your portable drill in a right-angle drill guide, you can drill perfectly perpendicular holes. Some models can be tilted to allow you to drill at an angle. Most also contain a bit stop setting so you can set precise drilling depths.

With the bit stop on the drilling guide set to 2 in. drilling depth, we drilled a series of overlapping holes inside each mortise outline to remove the waste wood **(See FIGURE H)**.

9 Square the walls of each mortise with a sharp wood chisel **(See FIGURE I)**. If possible, the width of the chisel should equal the width of the mortise (¾ in. in our door). The beveled edge of the chisel should face into the center of the mortise. After all the mortises are cut and squared off, test the fit of each tenon into the appropriate mortise. Generally, it's easier to make necessary adjustments by paring the tenon slightly with a file or sander. The tenons should fit into the mortise cleanly, with slight resistance.

• Assemble the door frame •

10 On a flat, sturdy work surface, dry-assemble the door rails and stiles **(See FIGURE J)**. Make sure the shoulders of all tenons fit flush against the rails. Measure the diagonals (the distance between opposing corners) and adjust the assembly until the diagonals are equal to make sure the door is square.

11 Once you're satisfied that all the joints fit together properly and the door can be squared up successfully, disassemble the dry assembly and prepare for glue-up. For best results, you'll need at least six to eight pipe clamps or bar clamps long enough to span the width of the door. Set the door stiles onto spacers to create room for clamps on the underside of the door. Apply glue to the tenons and to the mortises on one side and slip all four tenons into their mortises. Assemble the other side. Clamp the door frame together, alternating clamps above and below the door to distribute clamping pressure evenly **(See FIGURE K).** Use clamping pads or blocks between the clamp jaws and the stiles. Before the glue sets, measure the diagonals again and adjust the clamp pressure and positions until the door is square.

FIGURE J: Dry-fit the rails and stiles on a flat worksurface to make sure everything fits together properly. If adjustments need to be made, it's easier to trim the tenons than the mortises.

FIGURE K: Glue and clamp the door frame together, alternating clamps above and below the door to distribute clamping pressure evenly. Use scrap blocks between clamp jaws and the door stiles to keep the clamps from marring the stiles. Before the glue sets, measure the diagonal corners of the door—if the distances are the same, the door is square. If not, readjust the clamps to square the frame.

Spacers

FIGURE L: Use a drill mounted in a drill guide to bore ⅜-in.-dia. dowel holes all the way through the mortise-and-tenon joints. Be sure to slip a backer board underneath each dowel area of the door to prevent the bit from chipping and tearing the wood when it exits the back.

FIGURE M: Drive a pair of ⅜-in.-dia. oak dowels through each mortise-and-tenon joint. The dowels provide back-up protection in the event of joint failure.

FIGURE N: Glue up the ¾-in.-thick solid oak boards that will be used to make the raised panels. Arrange the glued-up boards so their wood grain will run horizontally when the panels are installed.

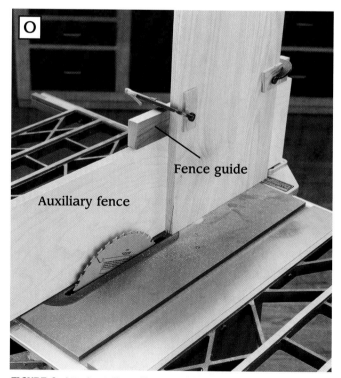

Fence guide

Auxiliary fence

FIGURE O: Attach a tall, auxiliary wood fence to the table saw fence. This will provide vertical support when machining the raised panels. Practice with test pieces of ¾-in. stock until you've found the combination of blade height and bevel that makes the desired cut (a 3-in. cutting height with a 10° bevel is shown here).

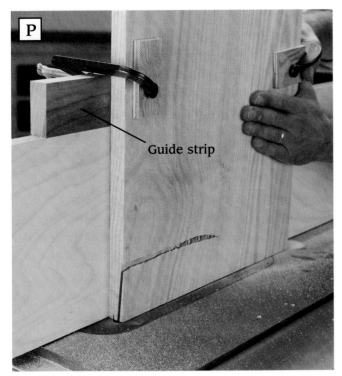

FIGURE P: Using an auxiliary fence and a guide strip clamped to the workpiece, feed each edge of one panel through the saw blade. The top of the blade should just break the outer face of the workpiece.

FIGURE Q: Cut raised profiles in the other side of each panel, using the same techniques, to complete the raised-panel cuts.

12 Allow the glue joints to dry. As extra insurance against joint failure, we pinned all the mortise and tenon joints with pairs of ⅜-in.-dia. oak dowels driven through each joint and glued into place. Using the drilling guide, drill a pair of ⅜-in.-dia. holes 1 in. away from the inside edge of each rail at each joint. Space the holes about 1½ in. from the top and bottom of each rail. Slip a backer board beneath the drilling areas before you drill all the way through the door frame—this prevents tearout when the bit exits the wood. Drill the dowel holes **(See FIGURE L).**

13 Cut sixteen 2-in.-long oak dowel pins, then apply glue to the pins and drive them into the dowel holes with a wood mallet **(See FIGURE M).** Stop driving each dowel when the end is about ⅛ in. away from the wood surface. Let the glue set until dry, then trim both ends of each dowel pin flush with the wood surface.

• Make the raised panels •

14 The raised panels for our door were cut from ¾-in.-thick oak panels we edge-glued together. Before gluing up panels, measure each opening and subtract ⅛ to ¼ in. The panels should be slightly smaller than the openings to allow for expansion. When arranging the panels for glue-up, make sure the grain is running horizontally. Joint all edges before glue-up. Glue up the panels **(See FIGURE N).** Let the joints dry overnight.

15 Rip-cut and cross-cut the oak panels to their finished dimensions. Scrape off any glue squeeze-out, then belt-sand or plane the surfaces until they're smooth and even.

16 To create the raised panels, we used a table saw set to cut a bevel at each panel edge. Setting up for the cuts takes a little trial and error. Each cut should start ¼ in. in on the panel's edge and taper toward the surface so the blade just barely exits the wood at the top, leaving a ridge about the thickness of the blade at the top of each cut. Setting the blade at a 3 in. cutting height with a 10° bevel worked on our saw with our stock. Make test cuts on ¾-in.-thick scrap until your saw is set to make the cut you want **(See FIGURE O).** For extra workpiece support, we attached a tall auxiliary fence to the table saw fence. To make the cuts, stand the workpiece on edge and clamp a guide block to the workpiece to ride along the top of the fence.

17 Feed the workpieces slowly through the blade, keeping them snug against the fence, and your hands and sleeves clear of the blade. Cut all four faces of each workpiece, then flip it over and cut the other four faces **(See FIGURES P and Q).**

FIGURE R: We mounted a double Roman ogee bit (inset photo) in our router table and used it to shape the edges of strips of oak. The strips are ripped to width to form the retainer strips for the door frame openings.

Push stick

FIGURE S: Rip-cut the trim into ¾-in.-wide strips on your table saw or band saw. Be sure to use a push stick to guide the strips over the saw blade.

• Make the retainer strips •

18 The raised panels and the glass light panel are held in the frame opening with ¾- × ¾-in. retainer strips mitered at the corners to form frames. For the door shown, you'll need a total of about 42 ft. of retainer strip. You can purchase premilled oak molding that will work for the retainer strips (base shoe or quarter-round), but we wanted a more decorative appearance so we decided to cut our own moldings. We mounted a double Roman ogee router bit with a ½-in.-dia. shank in a router table, then routed a decorative profile into the edge of several long strips of ¾-in.-thick oak stock **(See FIGURE R).**

19 Rip the edge-routed trim pieces to ¾-in. width on your table saw or band saw **(See FIGURE S).**

• Install the panels & glass •

20 Cut the retainer strips with 45° mitered corners to fit snugly inside the perimeter of each frame opening. Assemble and install a retainer frame on one side of each frame opening. Attach the retainer strips with glue and 1-in. wire brads driven into pilot holes. **(See FIGURE T).** Make sure the front edges of the retainer strips are flush with the door frame.

21 Turn the door over and lay both raised panels in their openings. Glue and nail in the retainer strips to hold the panels in place from this side of the door **(See FIGURE U).** Use the glue sparingly so that it does not come in contact with the raised panels; they should float freely between the retainer frames.

22 For best results, apply the finish to the door before installing the second retainer frame to secure the glass light panel. Sand all wood parts with 100-, 150- and then 180-grit sandpaper. We used a red mahogany wood stain to match the trim in the door opening our door was built to fit. For a topcoat, we used three coats of tung oil varnish. Be sure to stain and finish the unattached retainer strips for the glass panels as well.

23 We had a 21¾ × 29⅞ piece of ¼-in.-thick reinforced glass cut to size at a local glass shop. Reinforced glass contains a piece of plastic film layered inside the glass to resist breaking. To install the glass, we laid a thin bead of clear silicone caulk inside the first retainer strip frame, seated the glass into the caulk bed, then attached the finished retainer strip frame **(See FIGURE V).** To hang the door, see pages 112 to 113 for more information.

FIGURE T: Miter-cut the ends of strips of retainer molding at 45° to create a frame inside the door frame openings. Install frames on one side of the door in all three openings.

FIGURE U: Set the raised panels onto the attached retainer frames, then attach a second mitered frame over each panel to hold it in place. Avoid getting glue on the panel—it should float freely in the opening so it can expand and contract with changes in humidity.

FIGURE V: Sand and finish the door and retainer strips before installing the glass light panel. To provide a little cushion for the glass, we seated it in a thin frame of clear silicone caulk before attaching the second retainer strip frame.

Index